Ged Martin

Ged Martin lives in County Waterford, Ireland, and was formerly Professor of Canadian Studies at Edinburgh University. He has published widely on the history of Canada, Ireland, and Britain, including *Britain and the Origins of Canadian Confederation, 1837–1867* (1995). His *Favourite Son? John A. Macdonald and the Voters of Kingston, 1841–1891* won the Ontario Historical Society's 2012 J.J. Talman Award for the best book in the social, economic, political, or cultural history of the province. He is an Honorary Fellow of Hughes Hall, Cambridge, and an adjunct professor at the University of the Fraser Valley.

In the same collection

A QUEST BIOGRAPHY

JOHN A. MACDONALD

CANADA'S FIRST PRIME MINISTER

Ged Martin

DUNDURN
TORONTO

Editor: Britanie Wilson
Design: Jesse Hooper
Printer: Webcom

Library and Archives Canada Cataloguing in Publication

Martin, Ged
    John A. Macdonald : Canada's first prime minister / by Ged Martin.

Includes bibliographical references and index.
Issued also in electronic formats.
ISBN 978-1-4597-0651-4

    1. Macdonald, John A. (John Alexander), 1815-1891. 2. Prime ministers--Canada--Biography.
3. Canada--Politics and government--1867-1896. I. Title.

FC521.M3M37 2013   971.05'1092   C2013-900807-1

    2   3   4   5   17   16   15   14   13

Conseil des Arts
du Canada
Canada Council
for the Arts

Canada

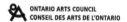
ONTARIO ARTS COUNCIL
CONSEIL DES ARTS DE L'ONTARIO

We acknowledge the support of the Canada Council for the Arts and the Ontario Arts Council for our publishing program. We also acknowledge the financial support of the Government of Canada through the Canada Book Fund and Livres Canada Books, and the Government of Ontario through the Ontario Book Publishing Tax Credit and the Ontario Media Development Corporation.

Care has been taken to trace the ownership of copyright material used in this book. The author and the publisher welcome any information enabling them to rectify any references or credits in subsequent editions.

J. Kirk Howard, President

Printed and bound in Canada.

VISIT US AT
Dundurn.com | Definingcanada.ca | @dundurnpress | Facebook.com/dundurnpress

Dundurn	Gazelle Book Services Limited	Dundurn
3 Church Street, Suite 500	White Cross Mills	2250 Military Road
Toronto, Ontario, Canada	High Town, Lancaster, England	Tonawanda, NY
M5E 1M2	L41 4XS	U.S.A. 14150

Contents

Acknowledgements

My research into the career of John A. Macdonald was assisted by a Government of Canada Faculty Enrichment Award. I record appreciation to conference and visiting speaker funds of Brock, Edinburgh, Fraser Valley, Galway, and Ryerson Universities. Kirk Howard encouraged me to write this book, and his colleagues at Dundurn Press have efficiently steered it to completion. Thanks are owed to many individuals, including Elizabeth and Robert Andrews, Ann Barry, Colin M. Coates, Vivien Hughes, Robin Jeffrey, J.K. Johnson, Barbara J. Messamore, Brian and Anne Osborne, Grace Owens, Simon J. Potter, Peter B. Waite, and Donald Wright.

Introduction

Only Make a Beginning

On July 1, 1867, John A. Macdonald became Canada's first prime minister. Confederation, as the process was called, split the existing province of Canada, formed in 1841, allowing its two sections, Upper and Lower Canada (Canada West and Canada East), to form the separate units of Ontario and Quebec. They joined New Brunswick and Nova Scotia to become the Dominion of Canada. A talented lawyer, efficient administrator, and prominent figure in Upper Canadian politics, Macdonald had played an important role in creating the new political union.

His family had arrived in Kingston, Ontario, when he was five years old, after the failure of his father's business in Scotland. They continued to struggle in Canada. At fifteen, he became a clerk in a law office, and worked his way to the top. Years later, a friend confided that he too wanted to become a lawyer, but doubted whether he had the time or resources to study. Macdonald offered sage counsel: "only make a beginning, and you will get through some way or other." He applied that philosophy to projects such as Confederation and the transcontinental railway, with a combination of determined optimism and practical caution that earned him the grudging nickname "Old Tomorrow." John A. Macdonald died in office in 1891 after leading the Dominion for nineteen of its first twenty-four years. By then, Canada had expanded to the Pacific and acquired three more provinces (Manitoba, British Columbia, and Prince Edward Island). Newcomers settling the prairies (the future Alberta and Saskatchewan) disrupted traditional lifestyles, and in 1885 some Métis and Native people rose in revolt. It was ironic that Macdonald's final years were overshadowed by the tragedy of the Riel uprising, since his political philosophy of deal-making compromise had been shaped by the shocking experience of Upper Canada's 1837 rebellion. Although he rarely spoke of his experience of serving in the government forces in that minor civil war, he learned an enduring lesson about the fragility of Canadian society.

Of course, Canada has changed since Macdonald's day. The title "Dominion" was no accident: Macdonald intended Ottawa to be the boss, with the provinces as subordinates, not federal partners. The centrepiece of his later years was the Canadian Pacific Railway, completed in 1885 to stiffen the transcontinental nation with a steel spine. Canada's rail network still handles bulk freight, but trains carry more tourists than travellers. The railway formed part of Macdonald's National Policy, the 1879 protective tariff that encouraged western Canadians and Maritimers to buy goods mainly manufactured in Ontario and Quebec, a structure finally discarded in the Canada-U.S. Free Trade pact of 1988. John A. Macdonald forged the Conservative Party as a powerful instrument to govern Canada by mobilizing support among both its English- and French-speaking citizens. But, after his time, the party generally failed to win support in French Canada. Political parties evolve new policies as circumstances change: the 1988 continental trade pact was struck by

The rising lawyer-politician, John A. Macdonald, about 1856.

the Conservative government of Brian Mulroney. Macdonald's Pacific Railway was a partnership between government and a heavily-subsidized private company; Canada's modern-day Conservative Party champions a free-market economy. John A. Macdonald's nineteenth-century blueprint cannot function as a straitjacket for twenty-first-century Canada.

Ruling Canada from Ottawa, squabbling with provincial premiers, protecting the country from the Americans — John A. Macdonald can seem a very modern figure. However, social and political values were often different to those of today. Politics was a man's game. Macdonald was encouraged to enter Parliament by his ambitious mother, Helen (Shaw), but his first wife, Isabella (Clark), who died in 1857, played no part in his campaigns and disliked his involvement. His second wife, Agnes (Bernard), who married him ten years later, was initially snubbed if she dared to offer her opinions. Ultimately, this tough-minded woman became his confidante, but she never made a political speech, nor indeed could she even vote. In 1885, Macdonald considered giving the franchise to women who owned property, but his agenda was conservative, not feminist: women did not vote in any federal election until 1917.

It was an era in which religion formed a public, almost tribal, badge. Until Macdonald solved the issue in 1854, Protestant denominations squabbled over the clergy reserves. A deep schism existed between Protestants and Catholics. Even Macdonald, a generally tolerant person, objected when his own son decided to marry a Catholic. He was first elected, in 1844, as a Protestant politician, backed by a fraternal organization, the Orange Order — fraternal to other Protestants, but hostile to Catholics. The governing alliance that he built from 1854 with the "Bleus," French-speaking conservative Catholics, strained his local powerbase, and in 1861 a section of Kingston Orangemen turned against him. In the province of Canada, the two sections were allocated the same number of seats in the Assembly. By 1860, the population of Upper Canada was surging ahead, and Confederation was partly designed to give its people a larger say in the running of the government: Ontario in 1867 received eighty-two seats, to Quebec's sixty-five. To modern ears, that sounds like democratic fairness, but the cry for "rep. by pop." was often a coded demand by Protestants for supremacy over Catholics.

Catholics and Protestants argued about schools, but they agreed on many issues that would be divisive today: Macdonald believed abortion "saps the very life blood of a nation" and called it a worse crime than rape. Almost everybody believed in capital punishment, that the State had the right to punish serious crimes by killing the offender. John A. Macdonald was the prime minister whose government confirmed the execution of rebel leader Louis Riel in 1885. That seems shocking: nowadays only the cruellest dictators use the death penalty to silence political opponents. But hanging was part of Macdonald's world. Aged twenty-two, he lost a case and his client died on the gallows. As attorney general (justice minister) before Confederation and as prime minister after 1867, Macdonald approved the executions of ninety-five men and two women, mostly sentenced to death for murder. Riel's death was controversial at the time, but we should assess Macdonald by the values of his era, not ours.

The sternly vengeful nineteenth century was surprisingly easy-going about the relations between business and the rough trade of politics. MPs received no salaries: there had to be some pay-off for taking part. Elections were violent and expensive, and serving in Parliament involved long absences in distant cities. Most politicians had business interests — hence politics was dominated by lawyers (like Macdonald himself) and merchants. They helped their ridings by boosting local companies and lobbying for public works. A candidate who could not enrich himself was reckoned too dumb to look after his riding. But there were limits: John A. Macdonald lost office in 1873 because he appeared to have sold the contract for the Pacific Railway to the Montreal magnate who had funded his election campaign the previous year. The charge was exaggerated, but it took him five years in opposition to shake it off. In the last two years of his life, the stench of corruption leaked out again: Macdonald died in office partly because he could not walk away.

"A British subject I was born," Macdonald proclaimed in 1891; "a British subject I will die." These sentiments of deference to a distant European homeland now seem embarrassing, as if his generation was trapped in colonial adolescence, too scared to accept grown-up nationhood. But there was hard-nosed reality in Macdonald's rejection of Canadian independence as "all bosh." In 1891, almost 5,000,000 Canadians lived alongside 63,000,000 Americans: Canada needed a powerful external protector to have any long-term chance of survival. Britain could not prevent an American invasion, but its mighty navy was a vengeful deterrent. Canadians needed to maintain an effective militia for local defence but, overall, it made sense to spend tax dollars on internal development, relying on the British to pay for warships. It was convenient, too, to accept a governor general sent out from "Home," and avoid the nuisance of presidential elections. Deriving authority from the Westminster Parliament ensured legal continuity, hence the British had some say in the shaping of Confederation. However, Canadians were not subservient to Britain. Canada, New Brunswick, and Nova Scotia had enjoyed local self-government since 1848, and the new Dominion set its own priorities. British manufacturers were outraged by Macdonald's National Policy: their taxes paid for Canada's naval defence, but their goods could not freely enter the Canadian section of the Empire. When Macdonald said he was proud to be British, he meant that he was determined to be Canadian.

In the unique circumstances of Confederation in 1867 Canada's first prime minister was appointed before the new Dominion's Parliament had been elected. Impressed by Macdonald's handling of the new constitution at meetings in London the previous winter, the British chose him for the job, elevating him above his contemporaries with the knighthood that made him Sir John A. Macdonald. To his admirers, the choice was obvious. Ontario, the largest and richest province, claimed the top job, and Macdonald was an efficient administrator and accomplished political manipulator. Unfortunately, Macdonald's appointment was resented by George-Étienne Cartier, his Quebec ally (and rival). Go-ahead Ontario voters generally voted for Reformers (Liberals, as they gradually came to be called). Far from speaking for Canada's largest province, as a Conservative, Macdonald belonged to a threatened species. Paradoxically, his big asset was his chief opponent, newspaper owner George Brown, a bully whose mighty Toronto *Globe* (now the *Globe and Mail*) denounced anybody who dared disagree with him. Calling himself a Liberal-Conservative, Macdonald welcomed Brown's victims, maintaining support in his own section by constant coalition-building.

John A. Macdonald's fondness for wordplay gives us a glimpse of how his mind worked. Once, Isabella's sister decorated a letter with a mysterious motto, a large capital "I" followed by "2 BU." Macdonald successfully decoded it as "I long — to be — with you." Evidently, he would have enjoyed text messaging. He also relished puns. Adulterating sugar was a more serious crime than murder, because it was a *grocer* offence. The Minotaur, the monster of Greek legend, fell asleep after devouring a maiden, because of "a great *lass he chewed*" (lassitude!). That horror dates from around 1864, when the same brain was designing the constitution of modern Canada.

John A. Macdonald had one weakness capable of destroying his career: an alcohol problem. To this day, he is often regarded as merely a genial drunk. For two decades from 1856, he occasionally took refuge from his problems — personal, political, and financial — in binge drinking, sometimes at crisis moments in Canada's destiny. But he was not permanently intoxicated, nor was Canada created in an alcoholic haze. Macdonald was a remarkably effective politician: as he said himself, Canadians preferred John A. drunk to George Brown sober. In the mid-1870s, he faced up to the issue and beat the bottle. His intermittent inebriation stemmed from pressures in his life that can be traced back to his childhood in Glasgow, Scotland, where he was born in 1815.

1

1815–1839
I Had No Boyhood

John Alexander Macdonald was born on January 11, 1815, in Scotland's industrial city of Glasgow. Most of its 150,000 people lived on the north bank of the Clyde, but Canada's future prime minister was born "in one of a row of stone tenement houses," part of a residential area south of the river — "tenement" was a Scots term for an apartment block. His parents were from the Scottish Highlands. Hugh Macdonald was a short man; Helen Shaw was both physically larger and four years older — an age gap that their son replicated in his first marriage. The couple had five children, the last born when Helen was forty. Margaret came first: "my oldest and sincerest friend," Macdonald called her sixty years later. There were two younger siblings, James and Louisa; another boy had died in infancy. Their mother possessed a driving willpower and a lively sense of humour, both of which she greatly needed. To her son John, she transmitted a determination to succeed in life — as well as his celebrated prominent nose. Helen spoke

Gaelic, but Scotland's ancient language was associated with back-wardness, and she did not to pass it on to her son.

Two contrasting stories survive from John A. Macdonald's early days. One shows him playing to an audience. To impress other children, the four year-old placed a chair on a table, climbed up, and delivered a speech, accompanied by vehement gestures. Unluckily, he overbalanced, fell, and gashed his chin. Macdonald's first recorded oration left him with a lifelong scar, which photographers generally painted out. He was probably imitating a fiery sermon from a Presbyterian preacher. Perhaps his parents considered a Church career for him, until a schoolmaster in Canada commented that the argumentative boy would make a better lawyer than minister. The second tale reveals an introspective side of young John's character. Taken for a walk through the busy streets, he became lost in the crowds, but was too young to explain where he lived. Eventually his father rescued him, and punished him. Such were the harsh standards of the time — and this is one of the few glimpses of Hugh in the story.

Glasgow was a boom town, heading for a bust, and Hugh Macdonald was one of the early casualties. When his small-scale textile-manufacturing enterprise failed, relatives blamed "the knavery of a partner," but he was no businessman, and there are hints that he drank too much: John A. Macdonald's alcohol problem was probably inherited. Financially ruined, the Macdonalds were forced to seek a new life overseas. In Helen's complex family network, two relatives might offer support. Her brother, James Shaw, had emigrated to Georgia, while a half-sister, Anna, had married a British Army officer, Donald Macpherson, and settled at Kingston in Upper Canada. Unfortunately, the Macdonalds were not the only members of the extended family in crisis. The children of another half sister, Margaret Clark, were orphaned in 1819.

The five Clark girls were bred for genteel life, and were more likely to find suitable husbands among Southern planters than in the pioneer world of Canada. The eldest of them, Margaret, twenty-two in 1820, led three of her sisters to Georgia. One of them, Isabella, then aged eleven, later became Macdonald's first wife. However, in childhood, she could hardly have known her five-year-old cousin well.

Another Clark daughter, Maria, fifteen in 1820, joined the Macdonalds to help rear their children, and travelled with the family to Canada. Although ten years his senior, Maria outlived Canada's first prime minister and became the source of memories of his childhood.

Emigration was often a lottery. If the Clarks had not been orphaned, the Macdonalds might have joined Helen's brother in Georgia (after all, Hugh knew the cotton trade). Instead of becoming a Father of Canadian Confederation, John A. might have served the Southern Confederacy, fighting to defend slavery in the American Civil War. Instead, the family headed for the Macphersons' in Kingston. Donald Macpherson had joined the British Army back in 1775, and risen to the rank of colonel, commanding the Kingston garrison when the Americans attacked in 1812. Now retired and a respected citizen, he had recently built a suburban mansion. The Macdonalds moved into his former downtown residence.

It is hard to assess the importance of John A. Macdonald's early childhood in Scotland. He visited relatives there on his first return trip to Britain in 1842, but rarely if ever travelled north from London on subsequent transatlantic jaunts. He was a Canadian Scot, reared among exiles. Most of his early friends were Scottish — but, later, so too were some bitter enemies. He picked up a local accent, even ending sentences with the characteristic Canadian "eh?" He once jovially remarked that although he had "the misfortune ... to be a Scotchman .... I was caught young, and was brought to this country before I had been very much corrupted." With his locker-room sense of humour, he sometimes joked about kilts. No true Scotsman would be so disrespectful.

The Macdonalds endured a squalid six-week voyage to Quebec. Packed with several hundred passengers, the *Earl of Buckinghamshire* was about the size of a modern Toronto Island ferry, or Vancouver's SeaBus. Its washroom facilities were two privies, each less than fifty centimetres square, handily located over the stern. Crammed into a sleeping compartment, 1.5 metres square and stacked with bunks, were the parents, four children, cousin Maria, and Macdonald's seventy-five-year-old grandmother, whom Helen refused to leave behind. (She barely survived the journey.) Even this cramped space was shared with another emigrant family. By the time they reached Kingston, in mid-July 1820, they had been travelling for three months.

With hindsight, emigration to Canada was John A. Macdonald's first step towards a notable destiny. At the time, it seemed a humiliation. His parents became determined that their son must succeed to compensate for their failure. Helen in particular insisted that "John will make more than an ordinary man." A family tragedy added to the pressures. In 1822, Macdonald's younger brother, James, was killed in an accident — "if accident it can be called," commented an early biographer, catching Macdonald's anger at the tragedy even sixty years later. One evening, the parents entrusted their sons to an ex-soldier called Kennedy. Preferring boozing to babysitting, Kennedy took the children to a bar and attempted to make them drink gin. When the boys tried to run away, Kennedy lost his temper and hurled James into the iron grate of a fireplace, causing internal injuries that killed him. This appalling experience left John A. Macdonald as the sole surviving son, bearing the full weight of his parents' hopes upon his young shoulders.

Kingston was then the largest urban centre in Upper Canada, but it contained only three thousand people, smaller than most modern country towns. New York State was just across the St. Lawrence, but the United States seemed remote — although the Macphersons vividly recalled Yankee bullets smashing into Kingston's timber fortifications back in 1812. The British Empire, on the other hand, was a very real presence, thanks to the redcoats of the imperial garrison: the young John A. Macdonald even dreamed of a career under the British flag in India. The town had been founded in 1784 by Loyalist refugees from the newly independent American republic, families like the Hagermans and Cartwrights who had made sacrifices for Britain — and coolly expected rewards in return. Kingston's elite accepted successful newcomers, especially Scots or Irish Protestants, men like merchant John Mowat, from Caithness, who settled in 1816; lawyer Thomas Kirkpatrick from Dublin, who arrived in 1823; and — a decade later — the medical doctor James Campbell, who came from Yorkshire via Montreal. The son of a failed immigrant, John A. Macdonald had to gatecrash this local elite. For all his fabled political charm, his sometimes fraught relations with Kingston's leading families reflected his marginal status.

After failing to establish a store in Kingston, Hugh Macdonald shifted forty kilometres west to the village of Hay Bay in 1824. Later, he moved to the Stone Mills (now Glenora) in Prince Edward County, to run the flour mill that gave the place its name. Although Hugh had no farming experience, he considered moving still further west, to try growing wheat. A neighbour tactfully steered him away from the project: nothing would grow beyond Port Hope because "the summer frosts kill everything." Decades later, Macdonald quoted that story against pessimists who doubted the potential of the prairies. In 1836, the Macphersons arranged a job for Hugh as a clerk in the Commercial Bank, Kingston's own financial institution, and the Macdonalds moved back to town. By then, his son had replaced him as the family breadwinner. Hugh, it was discreetly recalled, was "unequal to the responsibilities of the head of a family." John A. recalled that it had been his indomitable mother who carried them through the difficult early years in Canada.

John A. Macdonald was a bright child, "the star of Canada," as one of Hugh's drinking pals called him. Aged ten in 1825, he was sent to the Midland District Grammar School in Kingston, an academy that specialized in teaching Latin and mathematics, subjects which were the key to professional or commercial careers. (The school was less effective at teaching French, a language Macdonald never mastered.) For five years he shuttled between the town and his family home in the country, living in both, belonging to neither. This strange phase of his life would emphasize the dual aspect of his character — the competitive and secretive personality who manipulated charm to win friends. In Kingston, he lodged with a miserly landlady, spending his free time cadging food from the Macphersons. The genial old colonel became an alternative father figure. Donald Macpherson had risen from the ranks to defend Canada for the Empire in the War of 1812; John A. Macdonald would replicate his gallant career in politics.

In class, the son of a struggling country storekeeper competed with the sons of the comfortable local elite, who likely looked down on him. Opening a gymnasium in Ottawa sixty years later, Macdonald joked "when I was a boy at school I was fighting all the time, but I always got licked." He continued to be a star pupil, the boy the headmaster would summon to the blackboard to impress visitors with the school's mathematical teaching. But the unending pressure to succeed took its toll. Once, facing stressful examinations, young Macdonald ran away from school, arriving home unexpectedly, and close to a breakdown. He paid a high price for his elite schooling. "I had no boyhood," he once said in later years.

In the holidays, Macdonald imitated Colonel Macpherson by playing soldiers with his sisters, casting himself as their commander. Once, when Louisa ignored orders, he picked up a real gun and threatened to shoot her for disobedience. Fortunately, Margaret dissuaded him, for the weapon was loaded. She probably saved Macdonald's political career: a slaughtered sister would have been an electoral liability. Campaigning in the area sixty years later, Macdonald spoke nostalgically of idyllic days when he had run wild and barefoot, but in fact he did not belong around Hay Bay and Glenora any more than he did in town. His parents' well-meaning gesture of inviting local children to parties to welcome John home from school probably accentuated resentment against the "big-nosed Scotch kid." The girls mocked him as "ugly John"; the boys bullied him. One winter, Macdonald tried skating on Lake Ontario. Sneering at his spindly legs, a local lad upended him on the ice. On another occasion, a bigger boy pinned him down and rubbed Hugh Macdonald's flour into his untidy black hair. For their part, the country children considered the interloper to be vindictive and violent-tempered.

"From the age of fifteen I began to earn my own living," John A. Macdonald once recalled, bemoaning his lost boyhood. But in pioneer days, most youngsters worked by their mid-teens, and his puzzling comment suggests that he had bigger expectations.

As prime minister, he remarked that if he had received a university education, he would have made his career in literature. Perhaps this was just political image-making, but maybe his hothouse schooling was intended as a preparation for a college education. If so, the idea must have been to send him to Scotland, where universities accepted students in their mid-teens: planned colleges in Montreal and Toronto had yet to open their doors. A dream of higher education in Scotland might also explain why, in 1829, John was switched to a new Kingston academy, opened by a young Aberdeen University graduate. One other clue is revealing. In 1839, Macdonald was scheduled to speak at a fundraising meeting in Kingston, part of the campaign to establish Queen's University. He prepared an address on the importance of education but, when his turn came, he could not utter a word. It was John A. Macdonald's only failure as a public speaker: the subject evidently triggered complex emotions. The dashing of his hopes for a university education perhaps helps explain John A. Macdonald's drive to succeed in life.

In 1830, Macdonald entered the Kingston law office of George Mackenzie, and also lodged in his house. A kindly couple with no children of their own, the Mackenzies gave their charge some space to manage his life. Like many adolescents, Macdonald disliked getting up in the mornings. One day, unable to rouse him, Sarah Mackenzie closed off every chink of light in the lad's bedroom and left him comatose in pitch darkness. When he eventually shook himself awake and opened the curtains, the sun was setting. The problem did not recur.

Young Macdonald's sharp intelligence and a photographic memory impressed his boss and, late in 1832, Mackenzie sent him to manage a branch law office at Napanee, forty kilometres west of Kingston. Not quite eighteen and operating independently for the first time, Macdonald had to choose the personality he wished to project. Initially, he wrapped himself in professional dignity, perhaps emulating his father's prickly concern for status. Mackenzie criticized his "dead & alive" pomposity. "I do not think you are so free & lively with the people as a young man eager for their good will should be." John A. Macdonald kept that letter, which contained some of the best advice he ever received. He would become another George Mackenzie, not a second Hugh Macdonald.

At the end of 1833, another opportunity presented itself. His lawyer cousin Lowther Pennington Macpherson — the old colonel's son — was dying of a lung disease, and under medical advice to escape the Canadian winter. Macpherson needed Macdonald to run his law office at Hallowell, in Prince Edward County. George Mackenzie graciously released him, and Macdonald found himself ten kilometres from the family home at Glenora. But was Hallowell an opportunity or a trap? Macpherson reported August 1834 that his cough was worse. "God only knows how it is to terminate." Cousin Lowther would never return, but John A. Macdonald had no wish to be consigned to a country backwater.

Even in the 1830s, Hallowell was overshadowed by its neighbour, Picton. The young man appreciatively remembered as a "poor and friendless boy" supported a campaign to merge the two communities under a neutral name, Port William, in honour of King William IV. John A. Macdonald's first attempt at a negotiated union under the symbolic headship of the British Crown was a failure: ambitious Picton simply swallowed up its neighbour. Thirty years later, Macdonald successfully led a second such project, Confederation, on a continental scale. At Hallowell, Macdonald took his first steps in community activity, helping to found a debating club, and serving as secretary of the local school board. Keen to keep him in town, local business-men reportedly offered to finance him in his own law practice, but his ambitions lay elsewhere.

John A. Macdonald seemed on track to becoming George Mackenzie's junior partner. Mackenzie was planning a political career and would need a trusted lieutenant to manage his law office and his election campaigns in Kingston. Rejecting the political polarization which later provoked the 1837 rebellions, Mackenzie sought the middle ground, advocating precisely the moderate Conservatism that Macdonald himself later cham-pioned. But the partnership never happened. In August 1834, cholera swept across Canada. The terrifying disease could kill within forty-eight hours and George Mackenzie was one of its victims. For John A. Macdonald, it was suddenly important to return to Kingston and inherit Mackenzie's clients. His motiva-tion was not entirely cynical. The back roads of rural Canada were notoriously bad, and travel through country districts was only possible on horseback. Macdonald tried it — and fell, breaking his arm. In Kingston, lawyers sat in comfortable offices and waited for clients to come to them. Macdonald redoubled his efforts to qualify, and we have a glimpse of him sitting under a willow tree in a Hallowell garden, "studying intently" while small boys played leap-frog around him. He passed his exami-nations and, in August 1835, set up in business as an attorney in a cross-street off Kingston's central business district.

There is a mystery here. Born in January 1815, Macdonald was twenty when he opened his first law office — but the mini-mum age to practise was twenty-one. His birth had been formally recorded, in distant Edinburgh, but Canada had no registration system. Apparently, John A.'s father agreed to counter-sign a statement backdating his birth by twelve months: in later years, the year of his birth was often given as 1814. It seems the first formal act of John A. Macdonald's legal career was to commit perjury — a harbinger of his ruthless readiness to cut corners in later life.

The young adult John A. Macdonald was "slender, with a marked disinclination to corpulency." Even in his seventies, leading a sedentary life as prime minister, his weight just topped eighty kilograms (180 pounds or under thirteen stone) — light enough for someone who was five feet, eleven inches (180 centimetres) tall — well above the average of the time. But he did not use his height to overawe. Macdonald had a slight stoop, an inclusive gesture that put people at ease. James Porter, a Picton acquaintance, recalled spotting him on the streets of Kingston whenever he visited the town — and was flattered to be affably recognized: "he wouldn't wait for me to come and speak, but he would duck his head in that peculiar way of his, and come right across the street to shake hands." The greeting was informal, man-to-man: "Damn it, Porter, are you alive yet?" Macdonald claimed that he forgot only one face in a thousand, and his impressive memory for people he had only met briefly would win him devotees across Canada. He had absorbed George Mackenzie's advice to loosen up: "no client, however poor, ever came out of Mr. Macdonald's office complaining of snobbery."

His giant nose and unruly black hair contributed to an unforgettable face, but not a pretty one. When Louisa was congratulated on resembling her famous brother, she indignantly commented that he was the ugliest man in Canada. It was a face full of character, manipulated by "a consummate actor," with "a strong desire to please," who could easily "assume the role of the intensely interested recipient." In the early years of slow-exposure photography, sitters had to remain motionless for lengthy periods. Hence most nineteenth-century politicians glare at us, pop-eyed with tension. But even the earliest photographs of John A. Macdonald convey a lively, genial personality: one of his theatrical skills was his ability to hold a pose. Yet he was not merely playing a role. Macdonald's "wit and his inexhaustible fund of anecdote" infused every gathering that he attended. One critic remembered prime-ministerial dinner parties, where Macdonald carried on a serious conversation at one end of the table, while "telling risqué anecdotes to the guests at the other end."

As James Porter recalled, "there wasn't much fun that John A. wasn't up to." At Picton, he formed a mock order of chivalry, la Société de la Vache Rouge (Knights of the Red Cow). One Christmas, Macdonald brought the Knights to Glenora for the ceremonial enthronement of his mother as patroness, a paper knife serving as her sword of office. As master of ceremonies, John A. wisecracked his way through the proceedings until tears of laughter ran down Helen's face. "God help us for a set of fools!" she exclaimed. Years later, Macdonald told an astonished British statesman about an American vacation he had taken with two friends, in which they pretended to be strolling players. Calling at taverns, Macdonald played tunes, one of his companions pretended to be a dancing bear while the third collected coins from onlookers.

Macdonald enjoyed irresponsible pranks. On summer night in Kingston, he led a group of friends in bricking up old Jemmy Williamson's doorway, a stunt requiring a couple of hours of silent labour. From a hiding place, they threw pebbles at the bedroom window until Williamson came downstairs to investigate. A solemn Scotsman who believed in Hellfire religion, he thought he had been walled in as a punishment for his sins. An earlier joke was even less amusing. A Picton hotelier was notorious for driving his buggy at daredevil speed through the town. One night Macdonald slowed him down by building a barrier across the darkened street. The victim escaped unhurt, but his buggy was damaged and the horse badly injured. Worse still, suspicion fell on an innocent man: Macdonald confessed, but managed to get the affair hushed up. He was less fortunate when an altercation with a local doctor came to court, although the assault charge against him failed: punches had been thrown when the medical gentleman had dismissed the young law clerk as a "lousy Scotchman."

Macdonald was also engaged in serious activity in the adult world. He was elected to a junior office in Kingston's Celtic Society, with twice-yearly banquets including toasts damning Canada's "external and internal enemies" (Americans and radicals) and praising "the immortal memory" of James Wolfe, conqueror of Quebec. This organization embodied an important Scots network, from which he recruited his first law pupil, Oliver Mowat, son of a prominent merchant, magistrate, and Presbyterian Church elder. The two were active members of the Kingston Young Men's Society — Macdonald was president in 1837 — which debated political and religious questions. In 1836, he had voted in his first election, helping the Tory John S. Cartwright to defeat the Reformers in the nearby riding of Lennox and Addington.

John A. Macdonald's political opinions were formed in a highly confrontational period of Canadian history. "Tory" was the shorthand for Conservatives, while, after Confederation, Ontario Reformers adopted the name of their French-Canadian allies, *le parti libéral*, to become the Liberal Party of Canada. An election pitting Tory-Conservatives against Liberal-Reformers sounds familiar to modern Canadians, but the outward two-party system masked four political streams, two on each side, usually forming uneasy alliances. The extreme Tories believed in privilege, so long as it was privilege for themselves. However, they were a tiny minority (hence their nickname, the "Family Compact") who needed the votes of more moderate Conservatives, people like John A. Macdonald who supported British institutions and the development of Canada's economy. "I could never have been called a Tory," he later recalled, mocking "old fogy Toryism."

Their opponents were split too. Moderate Reformers admired Britain's system of parliamentary government, and wished to adapt it to enable Canadians to run their own affairs through a miniature copy of the Westminster Parliament — a system known as "responsible government." They were uncomfortable allies of the radicals, who admired American-style elective institutions, and sometimes sought to defy the Empire and join the United States. Two-party politics in Canada operated more like a four-cornered boxing match, with some of the sharpest political struggles happening, not between, but within, the main groupings. However, as divisive issues were resolved, such as the achievement of responsible government, moderates on both sides found more in common with their erstwhile opponents than with their quarrelsome friends — a strategy that John A. Macdonald exploited to occupy the middle ground in politics for two decades after 1854.

Unfortunately, this subtlety was lost on the governor of Upper Canada, Sir Francis Head, an eccentric British Army officer who naively believed that anyone who opposed his Tory supporters must be a Republican traitor. Governor Head enlivened the 1836 campaign by issuing colourful appeals to vote for the Union Jack. With the right to vote confined to property-owning British subjects, barely a fifth of adult males qualified (and no women). It was alleged that in 1836, veteran Reformers were thrown off the electoral rolls on shabby pretexts, while normally sleepy bureaucrats rushed out title deeds to government supporters — which was probably how young Macdonald acquired the hundred acres of wild land that entitled him to vote. Predictably, the Reformers were routed. Fifty-five years later, in his last desperate election campaign of 1891, Sir John A. Macdonald would resort to the same unsavoury combination of flag-waving and manipulation of voter rolls.

Head's election victory was overkill. The big losers in 1836 were the moderate Reformers, their strategy of patient argument shown to be powerless against Tory arrogance. The vacuum of opposition was filled by radicals with their big talk of fighting for liberty. As mayor of York, journalist William Lyon Mackenzie had proved a decisive administrator, even changing the name of Kingston's burgeoning rival to Toronto. But in futile opposition, his newspaper became increasingly reckless. With the British authorities struggling to suppress a national uprising in French Canada, Mackenzie's inflammatory language fanned rebellion among his supporters, in the hinterland of Toronto. December 1837 became one of the most traumatic months in John A. Macdonald's life.

The crisis of that month was not just political but professional and personal. Macdonald had quickly acquired a reputation as a clever courtroom performer, who could talk to juries of working men in language they understood. Once he described an assault by saying the defendant "took & went & hit him a brick." Few cases were as daunting as that of William Brass, an alcoholic hobo charged in 1837 with raping an eight-year-old girl, a crime that carried the death penalty. Although Macdonald was praised for his "ingenious" defence, it was perhaps too clever. His first line of argument, that Brass had been too drunk to commit a sexual act, collapsed when the victim gave harrowing testimony. The young lawyer's fallback position, that his client's alcohol problem was a form of insanity, also failed. Despite Macdonald's "very able" performance, Brass was found guilty and sentenced to die. His execution, on December 1, 1837, was horribly bungled. Brass was publicly hanged, from an upstairs window of Kingston's courthouse. The executioner miscalculated the length of the rope, and Brass crashed into his own coffin. Despite pleading that his escape was proof of his innocence, he was dragged back upstairs and choked to death on a shortened noose. We can only guess the impact of this failure on the twenty-two year-old Macdonald, whose client was widely believed to be the victim of a frame-up. A decade later, Macdonald became a political ally of W.H. Draper, who had prosecuted Brass. Draper occasionally teased the younger man, reminding Macdonald that he was such a smart lawyer that his client had been hanged. Bricking up Jemmy Williamson's front door was a huge joke, but losing a court case could send a man to a hideous death.

Within a week, John A. Macdonald was facing death himself. He had travelled to Toronto, probably on legal business, but perhaps carrying a last-ditch plea to save Brass. News of insurrection in Lower Canada encouraged William Lyon Mackenzie to attempt to seize the Upper Canada capital. The first blood was shed on December 4, 1837. Three days later, a thousand-strong government force marched up Yonge Street to attack the rebel headquarters at Montgomery's Tavern. The militia outnumbered the insurgents, and they had the advantage of two big guns. A few shells fired at the tavern proved enough to rout Mackenzie's untrained followers.

Marching close to the front of the column, just behind the two cannon, was John A. Macdonald. "I carried my musket in '37," he would say in later years, laconically telling Parliament in 1884: "I suppose I fought as bravely as my confreres." Yet he was reluctant to talk about that day when he had gone into battle. His close friend, J.R. Gowan, only discovered that they had been comrades in arms at Montgomery's while reminiscing on the fiftieth anniversary of the armed clash. John A. Macdonald took part, not because he had volunteered, but because all adult males had a duty to serve in the militia. They were called out for a few days of basic training each summer, but they were definitely not disciplined soldiers programmed to stand and fight. Because there were few casualties in that brief skirmish, historians rather belittle the episode. Yet it was a frightening experience for men who had never been under fire: Gowan recalled his "strong inclination to *run away*."

Because Macdonald hardly mentioned his experience, the 1837 episode has never been factored into his life story. It is noteworthy that he took part, and significant that he never boasted about it: a Conservative politician might have proclaimed that he had risked his life to preserve Canada for Queen Victoria. John A. Macdonald is often caricatured as an amoral and unprincipled operator, who struck deals and cut corners. But we should see him as somebody who knew that Canadian society was fragile, who had learned that the art of government involved avoiding conflict among its contrasting elements — Tories and radicals, Catholics and Protestants, English and French. As he put it in 1854, Canadians should "agree as much as possible" and that meant "respecting each other's principles ... even each other's prejudices. Unless they were governed by a spirit of compromise and kindly feelings towards each other, they could never get on harmoniously together." In a rare allusion to those traumatic events, in 1887 he called the rebellion era "days of humiliation," adding that "we can all look back and respect the men who fought on one side or the other, for we know there was a feeling of right and justice on both sides." The clash at Montgomery's had been part of "a war of fellow-subject against fellow-subject" which he preferred to forget — but, throughout his career, he remembered the lessons of 1837.

Macdonald was angry with the authorities for provoking the conflict. He curtly refused promotion in the militia, and boldly defended victims of the Tory crackdown on dissidents, showing a courageous commitment to fair play in the heated post-rebellion atmosphere. Eight Reformers from the Kingston area were charged with treason on dubious evidence; in 1885, as he pondered the case of Louis Riel, he recalled how he had "tripped up" the prosecution to secure their acquittal. A further fifteen prisoners decamped from military custody. In angry over-reaction, the garrison commander, Colonel Henry Dundas, concluded the storekeeper, Reformer John Ashley, must have connived in their escape. Embarrassed local magistrates quickly released Ashley from jail, but the irate victim hired John A. Macdonald to sue for wrongful arrest. This was courtroom drama, for Dundas, the heir to a peerage, would one day sit in the House of Lords — too elevated a personage to answer to an angry storekeeper and a raw young barrister. Army officers called to give evidence found themselves roughly cross-examined. The judge summed up in the colonel's favour, but the jury shocked respectable Kingston opinion and awarded Ashley $800 — huge damages for the time. For years afterwards, the outraged officers of the garrison displayed the ultimate disapproval of English gentlemen by refusing to invite Macdonald to dinner, "but John A. cared nothing for that."

Although internal rebellion had collapsed, Canada remained under external threat. In mid-November, a paramilitary force from the United States landed at Prescott, one hundred kilometres downriver from Kingston. They were counter-attacked by British regulars, disciplined soldiers who stood firm and shot straight. By the time the invaders surrendered, there were several dozen fatalities. The prisoners were taken to Kingston, where one local resident was appalled to discover that his own brother-in-law was among those captured. After two senior lawyers refused to help, he implored John A. Macdonald to provide a defence. There was little the young lawyer could do: the invaders were tried by court martial, and the resentful military refused to recognize the upstart lawyer who had humiliated their commanding officer. A grisly batch of hangings ensued, and Macdonald was called to death row, to draw up the bandit leader's will as he awaited the gallows.

"Macdonald's popularity was terribly strained by his defence of these men." But John A. Macdonald was playing for higher stakes than popularity. He was putting down a marker: the elite must accept him, and on his own terms. For their part, the city's power brokers decided to recruit him. Increasingly challenged by Toronto, Kingston needed to maximize its local talent. In June 1839, John A. Macdonald became a director of the Commercial Bank — the institution where his father worked as a clerk.

That autumn, the death of Kingston's mayor, Henry Cassady, provided further opportunities. Cassady's legal apprentice, seventeen-year-old Alexander Campbell — like Oliver Mowat, offspring of the local elite — transferred to Macdonald's tutelage in October 1839. At intervals through the next fifty years, Campbell would act as Macdonald's business partner, campaign manager, and political lieutenant, usually dazzled but occasionally horrified by the activities of his magnetic mentor. Mowat soon moved to Toronto, but Campbell remained the workhorse who could handle groups who sometimes distrusted John A. — from genteel Tories to intolerant Orangemen. Macdonald also succeeded Cassady as the Commercial Bank's official legal adviser, a position previously held by George Mackenzie. At the age of twenty-four, John A. Macdonald could now shift his focus away from fee-grubbing courtroom work towards the attractive world of business and corporate law. He was no longer "poor and friendless." Hothouse schooling, grinding apprenticeship, plus ability, determination, and charm had won him a seat at Kingston's top table. He was almost one third of his journey through life. Now he could map out how he planned to live the rest.

2

1839–1854
Idleness Is No Pleasure

John A. Macdonald was seriously ill for a time in 1840, and his health continued to cause concern during the next two years. His father's death, in 1841, added to his family responsibilities, and he was probably working too hard. However, as he remarked during his first overseas holiday, "idleness is no pleasure," and he planned to return to his career "with greater zest and zeal than ever." In his mid-twenties, various options loomed: marriage, expansion of his law firm, and maybe a launch into politics, to advance Kingston's business interests — and his own.

Canada was entering a new political chapter. The British government had decided to unite Upper and Lower Canada into a single province, confident that the predominantly loyal Upper Canadians would control the *habitants*, who had posed the major challenge to the Empire in 1837–38. Both sections of the new province would have forty-two seats in the joint Assembly, thus overcoming the inconvenient problem that Upper Canada's

450,000 population — half that of modern Nova Scotia — was 200,000 fewer than that of Lower Canada. However, Montreal, Canada's largest city at the time, was largely English-speaking, and Anglophones would control about a dozen Lower Canada ridings, ensuring a 5–3 majority of English over French in the united legislature. Responsible government — a Canadian ministry answerable to the local legislature — was ruled out. Rather, the British governor-general would work with the Assembly just as the president of the United States dealt with Congress, persuading it to vote the taxes needed to pay for government and choosing his own Cabinet, irrespective of party. This imperial thinking was deeply flawed. Proclaiming that the Union was intended to subjugate French Canadians (even their language was barred in the legislature) guaranteed that they voted defensively as a national block. Since the rival English-speaking factions continued to squabble, the thirty French votes virtually controlled the Assembly. The French-Canadian leader, Louis LaFontaine, formed an alliance with the Upper Canada Reformers and, within eighteen months, he forced his way into office.

At the first elections in 1841, Macdonald was campaign manager for Kingston's Conservative candidate, John Forsyth. Since the right to vote depended upon owning property, his legal knowledge was important, and he discharged his task "ably and zealously." Unfortunately, Forsyth narrowly lost to local businessman, Anthony Manahan. Normally, as an Irish Catholic, Manahan would have been a no-hoper but, in this unusual election, he was seen as the candidate of the governor-general, Lord Sydenham, who had just selected Kingston as capital of the united province. Indeed, when Manahan took a government job soon after, the city dutifully elected Sydenham's right-hand man, S.B. Harrison.

Early in 1842, John A. Macdonald sailed to England for an energetic convalescence. In London, he attended parliamentary debates, whetting his political appetite by watching the great statesmen of the Empire. A new invention, railways, made travel easy. He visited Queen Victoria's private apartments at Windsor Castle, toured the Lake District, and looked up relatives in Scotland. He bought law books in London, a ceremonial kilt in Edinburgh, and state-of-the-art kitchen equipment in Manchester. Macdonald had cash to spend partly because of huge winnings in a card game before he left Kingston — an episode that perhaps triggered a row with his mother, because he never gambled again.

There was probably a bigger item on his want list than kitchen equipment: prosperous and twenty-seven, he needed a wife. For a young professional man, finding the right partner was not just a personal choice. Marriages might not be made in heaven, but the couple usually belonged to the same religious denomination. In Kingston, now a town of six thousand people of all ages and many faiths, the range of potential brides was limited. A lawyer's wife should be a sophisticated lady, but Canada seemed overrun, as Oliver Mowat complained, with "unthinking, unintelligent young women." Respectable families often imported brides: Macdonald was twice married, but neither partner grew up in Canada.

Although Helen Macdonald was a possessive mother, she could hardly have programmed her adult son to marry his cousin Isabella. But she probably sowed the seed by praising the female Clarks. The capable Maria, who had accompanied the family to Canada, had married a Macpherson and settled locally. Margaret was now a widow in her forties, but two younger sisters still lived with her. Jane had health problems;

Isabella was six years John A.'s senior. Helen, who had married a younger man herself, probably brushed that aside. The Clark sisters had left Georgia and, in 1842, were living on the Isle of Man, a Crown dependency in the Irish Sea, where low taxes created a refuge for hard-up gentility. Sending their "warmest love," they persuaded Macdonald to visit their backwater. There he proposed to Isabella and was accepted. The bride arrived in Kingston the next year, and the couple were married on September 1, 1843: in Scots tradition, the Presbyterian ceremony was held in Maria Macpherson's drawing room.

Within two years, Isabella's health and her husband's career combined to create a serious problem in the marriage, although their mutual affection was obvious. Thanks to their transatlantic courtship, the couple may not have known one another well when they agreed to share their destinies. When they married, Macdonald was twenty-eight, and Isabella thirty-four — an unusual age combination, but not an insuperable barrier in adult years. Perhaps the Clark sisters had visited Maria from Georgia — but when? Ten years previously, Isabella would have been a mature young woman, John a gawky teenage law clerk. Their romantic reunion on the Isle of Man was perhaps their first encounter on equal terms. During their short courtship, Macdonald probably told his fiancée that he hoped to enter the legislature, which then met in Kingston — a few blocks from home. Unfortunately, by the time she arrived, Canada's capital had been transferred to Montreal: Macdonald's election in 1844 meant long periods of absence. Isabella was no trophy wife, but she perhaps felt herself a captive daughter-in-law, with her ambitious Aunt Helen as her husband's mother. She recalled her days in Georgia and yearned for space in her part-time marriage.

Soon after Macdonald's return from Britain, the provincial Parliament met for its second session, in September 1842. The new governor-general, Sir Charles Bagot, accepted arithmetical reality: LaFontaine's alliance with Robert Baldwin's Upper Canada Reformers controlled the Assembly and they forced the governor to admit their nominees to his Cabinet. As Bagot wearily concluded, theoretical argument about responsible government was pointless, because "virtually it exists." In a rearguard action, he retained some existing Cabinet members for their administrative skills, including Kingston's defender, S.B. Harrison. In 1843, Bagot's health collapsed, and he was succeeded by Sir Charles Metcalfe. A former governor in India and Jamaica, Metcalfe was used to giving orders, not taking advice. A clash with his Reform ministers was likely, and confrontation would mean elections for a new Assembly. At this point, John A. Macdonald fought his first campaign.

In March 1843, Macdonald was elected as a Kingston alderman. Five months earlier, he had become president of the local St Andrew's Society, which gave him opportunities to wear his ceremonial kilt, and firm up his support among the Scottish community. He also joined the Orange Order, a Protestant Irish fraternal organization, which in Canada transcended its national origins. Its powerful political machine underpinned his electoral organization in Kingston until the Orangemen quarrelled with him in 1860–61.

Macdonald was elected easily, but it was a fierce campaign. Since property qualifications allowed few men to vote, the excluded majority disrupted political rallies in protest. John A. Macdonald proved a skilled performer, exchanging wisecracks with hecklers until he gained the crowd's attention, and then launching into a serious speech. At his victory rally, a platform collapsed, plunging him into the snow and he joked about the ups and downs of politics. Forsyth, the Conservative candidate in 1841, had been a halting speaker and was too obviously the privileged product of the local elite. If the party wanted a standard-bearer who could reach out and win votes, this genial self-made lawyer might be the answer.

He became a key player in municipal affairs at a moment of crisis for Kingston. The city had benefited from its selection as Canada's capital. (The official term was "seat of government": as part of the Empire, Canada's true capital was London, England.) The influx of politicians and bureaucrats boosted the local economy, but the newcomers were critical of the city's poor accommodations, both for people and institutions. The municipality planned a huge city hall for use as Canada's parliament house — but the real objection to Kingston was not its lack of facilities, but its atmosphere. French-Canadians felt uneasy with its loyalism, Reformers disliked its Toryism. When the new ministers lost an important by-election, Kingston Conservatives (Macdonald included) celebrated so riotously that the legislators felt intimidated. In March 1843, a Cabinet committee recommended moving the capital to Montreal. Harrison tried to block the decision, but in September he admitted defeat and resigned from office. Early in November 1843, the Assembly ratified the move. Three weeks later, Metcalfe forced the Reformers out of office, but it was too late for Kingston. Civil servants had quickly packed their files and hurried downriver.

Having ousted the Reformers, Metcalfe prorogued (i.e., suspended) Parliament to silence their supporters. Although the governor general delayed the call until September 1844, everybody knew that elections would soon follow. Kingston's Conservatives needed to unite behind an acceptable candidate — but who? The front-runner was probably lawyer John S. Cartwright, son of a founder of Kingston, who already represented a nearby riding. But Cartwright sailed to Britain in March 1844 to plead with the imperial authorities to veto the move to Montreal, a fruitless mission which destroyed his health. Into the vacuum stepped John A. Macdonald.

Years later, Macdonald modestly explained that he was selected to "fill a gap," adding: "There seemed to be no one else available, so I was pitched upon." He also recalled that he made it a condition that he might serve only a single term. Perhaps this was a tactical concession to the hereditary claims of Kingston's first families: in 1873, he recalled that they had distrusted him as "an adventurer" when he broke into politics. In reality, he moved effectively to seize the nomination. In April 1844, 225 Kingston citizens signed a requisition asking him to run — a well-organized show of strength. Macdonald responded by stressing that the signatories included "men of all shades of political opinion," highlighting his ability to reach out to uncommitted voters. He agreed "to lay aside all personal considerations" and run. Some Tories likely resented giving this upstart a free pass into Parliament for, in September, Macdonald staged a pre-emptive strike. He called a public meeting and asked whether his supporters might "now prefer to select another candidate." The outcome was a unanimous endorsement, with the intimidating pro-Macdonald chairman, old Jemmy Williamson, practically defying anybody to break ranks. Happily, Williamson did not know that Macdonald had once bricked up his doorway.

In his campaign, Macdonald waved the British flag: "the prosperity of Canada depends upon its permanent connection with the mother country," implying that Reformers were disloyal. He dismissed "fruitless discussions on abstract and theoretical questions of government," insisting that, as "a young country," Canada should "develop its resources." He backed schemes such as a plank road to the Ottawa Valley, to "make Kingston the market for a large and fertile, though hitherto valueless country." There was no hidden bonanza waiting in Kingston's rocky hinterland but, decades later, Macdonald would push Canada's westward expansion with equal optimism.

He emphasized his local credentials, promising "to advance the interests of the town in which I have lived so long and with whose fortunes my own prosperity is linked." For John A. Macdonald, politics was an extension of business. On September 1, 1843 — by whimsical coincidence, his wedding day — he signed a three-year partnership agreement with Alexander Campbell. Campbell would run the law office while Macdonald worked for Kingston in Parliament. Over the next two decades, Macdonald secured charters for twenty-five local projects, one of which, the Trust and Loan Company, a farm mortgage bank founded in 1843, would become a mainstay of his income. When he proclaimed that it was "alike my duty and my interest to promote the prosperity of this city and the adjacent country," John A. Macdonald meant what he said.

There was another, unstressed, plank in his campaign. Macdonald ran as a Protestant candidate against the Catholic, Anthony Manahan, claiming that he would be "hard run by the *Papishes*," a mildly offensive nickname for Manahan's Irish supporters. In fact, Macdonald won handily, by 275 votes to forty-two. However, he had lost the straw vote taken at the "hustings," the rowdy public nomination meeting, in which anybody could take part. In his early election campaigns, he invariably lost on the hustings but went on to triumph among the qualified voters: as the franchise widened, so his majorities fell. John A. Macdonald was elected by Kingston elite, not by the Kingston masses — but the bank clerk's son had shouldered his way to prominence. The riding might not remain as rock-solid as it appeared.

For Helen Macdonald, as she proudly watched the new member for Kingston board the steamer to Montreal, her son's election to Parliament likely closed the quarter-century of humiliation caused by her husband's bankruptcy in Glasgow. But Macdonald's wife was absent from the dockside. Life was going badly for Isabella, and we must probe the mystery of her health. We hear her voice from just two surviving letters, both probably written under heavy medication: "my head is very confused, & I am not sure what I say," she confessed in one of them. Some male historians have implied that she was a selfish airhead whose hysterical self-pity dragged down her husband's career —even driving him to drink. However, Isabella Macdonald suffered real pain, likely caused by trigeminal neuralgia, pressure on the facial nerve from enlarged blood vessels that causes a stabbing pain in the face. Often called the "tic" (the name Macdonald used), the condition interferes with normal activities, such as eating, sleeping, and kissing. In Isabella's case, it sometimes produced total physical collapse. Driven to desperate remedies, she became dependent upon pain-killing opium. Even if perhaps she manipulated her condition to gain control over her own life, her agonies were genuine. Macdonald's sister Margaret reported Isabella's "inability to take care of herself," adding that "poor John however willing" was "nearly as useless as a child" in looking after her.

In the summer of 1844 the Macdonalds had vacationed at New Haven, Connecticut. Isabella was not only determined to return the following year but also to spend the 1845–46 winter in Georgia, although a severe attack in July left her so exhausted that a Kingston doctor feared she would die. "It may be days — nay weeks — before she has rallied sufficiently to attempt any journey," Macdonald wrote despairingly. But Isabella aimed to get as far away from Canada as possible, and for as long as she could. Within a week of the crisis, she was carried to the Oswego steamboat and the couple started across Lake Ontario for New England. Her exhaustion was so "dreadful" that Macdonald feared his wife "would die on the deck." Yet, "strange to say her health and strength seemed to return" the further she travelled from Kingston. In October, Macdonald escorted her on the harrowing journey south. Even though Isabella was carried everywhere, exhaustion often forced her "to have recourse to opium." However, she indomitably insisted on pressing on: Isabella was not the weak heroine of melodrama. Fond of wordplay, Macdonald called her a "*Shero*," who "manfully" resisted her affliction. It took three weeks to reach Savannah, where he enjoyed his first taste of peach brandy, but early in December he had to return to Canada.

Macdonald left his wife behind at a time when the United States threatened war against Britain. On December 2, 1845, President James K. Polk aggressively demanded that the British clear out of the Pacific Northwest, the fur-trading region hitherto shared between the two countries. He also insisted that there must be "no future European colony or dominion … planted or established on any part of the North American continent." The Oregon crisis was resolved by dividing the territory along the forty-ninth parallel, but for several months there was a danger that Isabella would be stranded behind enemy lines. From Kingston in February 1846, Macdonald forlornly hoped his wife "may yet be restored to me, in health, strength and spirits." In fact, Isabella would be absent from Canada for three years.

If the new member for Kingston was risking his domestic happiness to sit in Parliament, he displayed a surprisingly low political profile, hardly speaking during his first two sessions. Macdonald entered Parliament at a toxic moment. Governor Metcalfe's narrow election victory was almost entirely based upon an English-Canadian majority. The result was a divided country and a weak government. John A. Macdonald spent the next decade learning the lessons of 1844. Ironically, Metcalfe's victory had proved Bagot's point: arguing over responsible government was pointless, for Canada was now governed by the dominant grouping in the Assembly. W.H. Draper, the governor-general's right-hand man, was effectively premier. Draper's precarious ministry needed Macdonald's vote, not his voice.

Keen to promote the interests of Kingston, John A. Macdonald avoided making enemies. Indeed, his most serious clash was with an arch-Tory, W.H. Boulton, who threatened him with a duel for allegedly slandering his family dynasty. (Duelling was going out of fashion, so it was safe to issue the threat.) In 1846, Macdonald secured a charter making Kingston a city, but his main interest was his mortgage business. The Trust and Loan Company's plan to lend money to farmers was hampered by Canada's Usury Laws, which capped interest rates. Well-intentioned but short-sighted, the Usury Laws gave Canadians no incentive to save, and made the province unattractive to overseas investors. Macdonald's strategy was to bypass the obstacle, by seeking an exemption permitting his own company to charge higher rates — which he eventually achieved in 1850.

"I like to steer my own course," Macdonald assured his family, but he was ambitious for office. As the danger of war with the United States receded, so a new threat to Canada came from Britain itself. Late in 1845, the imperial government announced the end of the Corn Laws, the preferential tariff that enabled Canadian farmers to export their wheat to Britain at lower import duties than their American rivals. Cheap bread was needed to stave off revolution in Britain's booming industrial towns and among the starving people of Ireland. In effect, Britain turned to the United States for its food. The repeal of the Corn Laws was followed by the end of protection on timber. In Canada, farmers, millers, loggers, and ship-owners faced ruin. Some feared Britain might abandon Canada altogether. The province needed ambitious politicians who would develop its resources.

In June 1846, Premier Draper decided he needed a minister with "activity of mind and familiar with business details" to clean up Canada's inefficient land-granting agency: Macdonald was the obvious choice. The governor general shared Draper's "very high opinion" of the thirty-one-year-old member for Kingston. Unfortunately, his appointment was prevented by the venomous split between Tories and moderate Conservatives, "selfishness" versus "patriotism" in Draper's vocabulary. Forced to appease the diehards, he appointed the even younger John Hillyard Cameron instead. Toronto and privilege had shouldered aside the self-made lawyer from Kingston. For twenty years, Cameron remained Macdonald's rival in the Conservative party.

Macdonald made his ambitions clear when he renewed his law partnership with Alexander Campbell in September 1846 for a further three years. Campbell received a larger share of the profits — and would be paid still more if Macdonald accepted political office. In December, Draper made Macdonald a Queen's Counsel. This promotion to senior legal rank allowed him to charge higher fees, and to use a junior barrister — Campbell of course — as his gopher in court cases. If Macdonald quit Parliament, he would have gained something from his time in politics. If he stayed, he was marked out as a potential attorney-general (justice minister). An angry Toronto newssheet denounced his elevation as "another deep insult offered to the Canadian people": the mottoes "corruption" and "incapacity" should be sewn on his new silk gown. The twice-weekly *Globe* was a minor nuisance, run by a young Scotsman called George Brown. Brown belonged to a breakaway Presbyterian church which delighted in denouncing sinners — a strategy incompatible with building political alliances. But, within a decade, the *Globe* became the most powerful newspaper in Upper Canada and Brown's the loudest voice in the Reform party — with Macdonald the special target for his venom.

Macdonald perhaps never saw the *Globe*'s first attack on him. His wife had travelled north from Georgia but was still reluctant to return to Kingston. The couple arranged to celebrate Christmas 1846 in New York, and celebrate they certainly did. Isabella soon discovered that, at the age of thirty-seven, she was expecting her first child: in her weakened state, she might not survive childbirth. Although pregnancies were managed by female relatives, Macdonald briefly considered dropping out of Parliament. However, he decided to return to Montreal for "the last act of my short political career," a renewed attack on the bigoted Tories who made the Conservative party "stink in the nostrils of all liberal minded people." In fact, he was appointed to Cabinet. He claimed to be "quite taken by surprise," but Draper's comment — "Your turn has come at last" — suggests Macdonald had pressed his claims. The new governor general, Lord Elgin, described Macdonald as "a person of consideration" among the moderate Conservatives whose appointment would strengthen the ministry. Critics pointed to his lack of experience and his low profile in Parliament: the *Globe* loftily dismissed him as "*harmless*," a judgment it soon revised.

Becoming a Cabinet minister at thirty-two was an achievement. Office-holders were styled "Honourable" for life: he was now the Hon. John A. Unfortunately, Macdonald had joined a failing government. Elections were due and, since Lord Elgin was under orders from Britain to be neutral, the Conservatives had no chance of repeating their narrow victory of 1844. As Macdonald recalled years later, "we went to a general election knowing well that we should be defeated." But for a young politician, it is a good long-term investment to join a government facing defeat: in the opposition years that follow, the novice can grow into a party heavyweight. Both Laurier and Mackenzie King founded their future careers on joining short-lived Cabinets.

Macdonald was appointed receiver-general, responsible for collecting government revenue. However, the only proposal that he put to Parliament dealt with university funding. His scheme planned to split funds allocated for higher education among four small Church-run colleges, which together catered for only a few dozen students. Macdonald's interest in the issue probably reflected his own regrets at his incomplete education. Dividing the funds appealed to his sense of fairness, although it helped that two of the four beneficiaries, Presbyterian Queen's and Catholic Regiopolis, were located in Kingston. Unfortunately, Macdonald's compromise collapsed when the Tories demanded all the money for the Anglicans.

Macdonald then rushed to New York for the birth of his son. Isabella suffered so much that her obstetrician tried a risky new treatment: she became one of the first women in the world to have the benefit of anaesthesia in childbirth, a process only pioneered a few months earlier. The technique was still so experimental that the medical team would not risk making Isabella unconscious in case they could not revive her: "from time to time, enough was administered to soothe her considerably." Isabella was so weak after her thirty-seven hour labour that forceps were used to deliver "a healthy & strong boy." In a brisk allusion to her sister's opium addiction, Maria Macpherson commented that it was no wonder the baby was very thin, "seeing he had been living on *pills* so long." Named "John Alexander" after his father, the child also inherited his famous nose. Maria whisked him back to Kingston to be cared for with her own brood. In an age of high mortality, the survival of both mother and child was a triumph — a point bizarrely driven home when Isabella's obstetrician suddenly died four weeks later. Despite Macdonald's intentions to stay in New York, he was soon forced to leave his "agitated" wife and return to his "solitary & miserable" life in Montreal. Worse still, her new doctor believed that Isabella's problems were psychological and sought to boost her confidence by persuading her to walk the length of her bedroom. She collapsed totally, and did not muster the strength to return to Kingston for a further nine months. Meanwhile, Macdonald's mother suffered a series of strokes, stretching the family womanpower to the limits. Forced to hire nurses for Isabella, Macdonald wrote that "we are in a nice mess."

But Canada's problems took priority, and the province needed its receiver-general at his desk. In the fall of 1847, an international banking crisis threatened government finances. Macdonald notified London banks of Cabinet's decision to raise the interest rates on Canadian bonds, thus giving himself useful name-recognition in the world's leading financial centre. The elections followed, and Macdonald no longer talked of only serving a single term.

Not only did he mobilize Kingston's Orangemen against a challenge from Tory Thomas Kirkpatrick, himself an Irish Protestant, but he also attempted to woo the city's Catholic bishop. Macdonald was handily re-elected, but the Reformers triumphed across the province. Macdonald's colleagues remained in office as caretakers until the new Assembly met in March 1848 and deposed them. Oddly enough, this graveyard shift witnessed an intense period of activity, the foundation of Macdonald's reputation for efficient administration. During the election campaign, he had switched portfolios to become commissioner of Crown Lands, and now he launched a whirlwind attack on its somnolent bureaucracy. The Trust and Loan Company needed reliable title deeds to issue mortgages, and delays in paperwork at Crown Lands were bad for business.

Macdonald's brief ministerial career was the prelude to six years of powerless opposition: as he confessed to an importunate constituent in 1849, "I have no influence whatever." Yet, despite domestic, professional, and political problems, he remained in Parliament. In June 1848, Isabella returned to Kingston, bearing the journey from New York "wonderfully well." To create personal space for his wife, Macdonald rented a house on the edge of Kingston, where the cooling breeze off Lake Ontario perhaps triggered a resurgence of her facial tic. Isabella ran the household from her bedroom. Having lived on a Georgia slave plantation, she was tough on servants: Macdonald nicknamed her the "Invisible Lady."

A happy and alert child, "John the younger" was cared for by a nurse but spent hours energetically playing with toys on his mother's bed. Isabella confessed to her sister: "my very soul is bound up in him.... did I not purchase him dearly?" The little boy was "in good health" when his first birthday was celebrated in August 1848. Seven weeks later, he was dead. One account mentions a fall, another convulsions: perhaps he tumbled from Isabella's bed and sustained head injuries? Of course, his parents never fully overcame their grief. Moving house in Ottawa in 1883, Macdonald's second wife discovered a mysterious box of toys: her husband quietly identified them as "little John A's." Isabella became trapped in a cycle of grief, pain, opium, and prostration. She was greatly distressed when her husband travelled to Montreal for the February 1849 parliamentary session — but Macdonald insisted that his attendance was "a matter of necessity."

Although he maintained his low profile, the 1849 session became a landmark in Macdonald's career. The new Reform ministry proposed to pay compensation for damage caused by government forces in Lower Canada during the 1837–38 rebellions. Convicted rebels were excluded — but very few insurgents had actually been prosecuted in those troubled times. Sympathy for the rebels had been widespread among French Canadians, and paying off claims for damage was a form of peace process, drawing a line under a tragic episode. But Tories violently objected to compensating the disloyal and embarked on a high risk strategy of reckless protest, designed to force the British government to intervene and restore them as Canada's natural rulers. Macdonald denounced the compensation proposals as "most shameful," and almost fought a duel with a Reform minister. But, as in 1837, he disapproved of extremism and fell silent as the temperature rose dangerously. Even amidst the cauldron of party hatred, he needed to pass technical legislation for the Commercial Bank.

In April 1849, he secured leave of absence from the Assembly for "urgent private business," probably another crisis in Isabella's health. He was lucky to get away from Montreal. On April 25, the city's anglophone mob burned down the parliament buildings. Macdonald condemned their behaviour, although he also blamed ministers for provoking popular anger. Arrogant and violent, the Tories had gone too far. Some even showed the hypocrisy of their vaunted allegiance to Queen Victoria by threatening to join the United States. The Conservative Party needed urgent reconstruction.

As a punishment, Montreal ceased to be Canada's capital. Parliament would meet first in Toronto and then go to Quebec City for five years. Macdonald insisted that "the system of alternate Parliaments would never do": Canada needed a permanent capital and Kingston was an attractive compromise. A new organization offered a way of rebuilding the party and boosting the city. In July 1849, 150 delegates gathered there for Canada's first political convention, to launch the British American League, which aimed to broaden Conservative support with new policies. Macdonald was a backstage organizer: as the *Globe* remarked, "he never says much anywhere except in barrooms." His aim was to create a new party organization, while demonstrating that Kingston's City Hall could host Canada's Parliament. As Macdonald hoped, the convention "put its foot on the idea of annexation." However, he displayed no enthusiasm for the League's alternative policy, the union of British North America, an early proposal for Confederation.

At forty, Isabella was expecting a second child. A painful and sleepless pregnancy was exacerbated by grief at the death of her sister Jane in November 1849, but the following March she gave birth to a son, Hugh John. "I never expected another," Macdonald admitted. To add to the pressures upon him, in September 1849, Macdonald lost his law partner. Alexander Campbell admired his mentor but he could not cope with

Macdonald's casual business practices. Although working relations with Campbell subsequently improved, the breach of 1849
never completely healed. Four months later, Macdonald likened
himself to "a thief on a treadmill" as he tried to maintain his
practice single handed until he could find a new partner. To save
money and escape unhappy memories, the Macdonalds moved
back into town. Isabella's health was worrying and expensive: for
a time, she was so weak that she was "unable to raise her hand to
her head." A medical bill for fourteen months in 1850–51 shows
that her doctor visited 132 times — a home call every three days
— at a dollar a consultation.

Over the next five years, before his return to office in
1854, Macdonald's priority was to strengthen his finances. He
achieved some short-term success, but at the price of long-range
problems. In 1850, he persuaded the Assembly to exempt the
Trust and Loan Company from the Usury Laws so that it could
charge higher interest rates. Macdonald promptly crossed the
Atlantic to recruit British investors. Calling him "a respectable
man and tolerably moderate in his views," Lord Elgin helped
Macdonald make contacts in London. Effectively, the Canadian
operation was converted into a financial branch-plant under
British control, giving Macdonald valuable experience in dealing with the elite who ran the Empire. The company's Canadian
headquarters remained in Kingston, where Macdonald was
returned by acclamation in the 1851 election. For the rest of
his life, Trust and Loan Company business helped subsidize his
political career.

Unfortunately, John A. Macdonald was less successful as a
speculator. His preferred strategy was to make a down-payment
on a block of land and quickly sell it at a profit, settling the balance of the purchase price from the proceeds and pocketing

the gain. In a spectacular deal in 1852–53, he invested a $1,000 deposit to secure land worth $5,060, which was soon sold for $9,400 — $4,360 profit for a thousand dollar outlay! Naively, Macdonald assumed that Canada's property bubble would continue, predicting in 1853 that "without exertion, I will be next year a rich man." In fact, two years later, he admitted that he was so over-extended that he could barely meet the instalments on his purchases, and begged creditors not to press him for money. He was naively over-optimistic in his hopes for a quick buck, buying land in Peterborough, Lindsay, and Owen Sound, prosperous communities but hardly boom towns. He owned 175 building lots at Guelph, a town of two thousand people, but by 1868 had sold fewer than a quarter of them. Even in dynamic Toronto, he was still paying city taxes on vacant sites decades later. He survived financially thanks to a growing overdraft from Kingston's Commercial Bank, although his duty as a director should have included asking hard questions about its indulgent business practices.

For an ex-minister, Macdonald seemed inconspicuous in Parliament: not until 1852 did he act like an opposition front-bencher, relentlessly criticizing the government. However, he championed one explosive issue. In 1848, the Reform ministry established a commission to investigate the Toronto *Globe*'s charges of cruelty in Kingston Penitentiary. There was certainly a case to answer, but it was a mistake to appoint the *Globe*'s masterful proprietor George Brown as the enquiry's secretary. Warden Smith, the target of Brown's denunciations, turned to his friend John A. Macdonald, who campaigned for another enquiry — into Brown's conduct. This was dangerous ground. Brown was a very sensitive bully, who smarted under criticism. Reform ministers rejected John A. Macdonald's annual demand: in 1851, he mocked their "cowardly fear of George Brown."

Among Upper Canada Reformers, the underlying split between radicals and moderates was revived by the "Clear Grits," whose rock-hard principles demanded American-style elective institutions. When the 1851 census showed that Upper Canada now had slightly more people than Lower Canada, they also demanded representation by population, "rep. by pop." for short. The issue flared in 1853, when the Assembly was enlarged from eighty-four seats to 130 — but still equally apportioned, sixty-five from each section. Upper Canada was booming not only demographically but economically: why, demanded the Grits, should the section paying the most taxes tolerate a veto from backward French Canada? Their outcry made life difficult for their francophone counterparts, the Rouges, as most Lower Canadians rallied to the moderate Bleus. With responsible government secured, the Bleus felt increasingly uneasy at being in political partnership with the Grit-dominated Reformers.

Throughout his opposition years, John A. Macdonald struggled to re-brand his party, even calling himself a "progressive Conservative," a name the Tories only adopted in 1942. Occasionally he despaired, once telling Campbell that the party was "nowhere, damned everlastingly." However, as the 1854 election approached, moderate Upper Canadian Reformers, followers of Premier Francis Hincks, sought to break with the uncomfortable Grits and find new allies. Hincks had personally profited from insider political knowledge — "rampant corruption," Macdonald had called it. But even if he did not survive in office, Hincks would act as king-maker — and he disliked Brown's dictatorial style.

The issue of the clergy reserves potentially blocked a Conservative-Hincksite coalition. In 1791, the British government had reserved one-seventh of the unsettled land in Canada — mainly in the upper province — to support the Anglican Church. In 1840, the reserves had been shared among several sects, but Grits wanted to end all State involvement in the financing of religion and transfer the entire land bank to the community. John A. Macdonald mocked the thought of "those worthy people in the Kingston Penitentiary" paying for their own prison chaplains. However, it was not an issue that he cared about deeply, and he recalled that anger against the clergy reserves had helped provoke rebellion in 1837. In June 1854, the Conservative caucus decided that if Upper Canada voted for secularization they would not resist. Reality was accepted even by Sir Allan MacNab, whose Tory rantings had been blamed for the Montreal riots.

John A. Macdonald had travelled a long way since 1849, when he had supported the slogan "no French domination." He accepted the necessity to "make friends with the French" and "respect their nationality." "Treat them as a nation and they will act as a free people generally do — generously. Call them a faction, and they will become factious." Moving the capital to Quebec City in 1852 had helped him get to know French Canadians: even if he barely spoke their language, he enjoyed their conviviality. Early in 1854, he predicted that a new government would be formed after the elections, "and from my friendly relations with the French, I am inclined to believe my assistance will be sought." It had taken him ten years to unlearn the toxic lessons of 1844. John A. Macdonald's second decade in public life would explore the limitations of partnership politics in a divided province.

3

1854–1864
The Dreary Waste of Colonial Politics

In September 1854, John A. Macdonald became attorney-general West (Upper Canada justice minister) in a coalition Cabinet of Conservatives, Hincksites, and Bleus, under the premiership of Sir Allan MacNab. Over the next decade, he rose through Canada's factional coalitions, then slipped backwards until he faced marginalization in what, in 1864, he called "the dreary waste of Colonial politics."

Reformers agreed to serve under MacNab, the archetypal fossil Tory, and MacNab himself was prepared to join with French Canadians, whom he had denounced as rebels, because a sudden revolution had plunged Canada into the age of steam. MacNab himself had redefined his politics as "railways." In 1850, there had been a few kilometres of track near Montreal. By 1856, railways snaked across the entire province. The centrepiece was the 500-kilometre Grand Trunk, planned to link Toronto and Montreal. Political pressure forced the Grand Trunk to extend eastward to

Lévis, opposite Quebec City, and also west to Sarnia, in wasteful competition with the Great Western, connecting Hamilton and Windsor. Two north-south lines were also important. A spur from Brockville encouraged backwoods Bytown to adopt a grander name. Rejecting the satirical alternative of "Byzantium," Bytown became "Ottawa" in 1855. Toronto's Northern Railway to Georgian Bay inspired the *Globe* with visions of a western empire to the Rocky Mountains. The new railway age required broader political alliances, thus prompting unlikely coalitions.

There were casualties in Canada's sudden steam revolution. Officially the Grand Trunk was a private company, but rapid construction wrecked its finances and effectively it was funded by Canadian taxpayers. Communities suffered if the railway bypassed them. With no interest in feeding lake traffic, the Grand Trunk ran its line around the back of Kingston: its refusal to build a station on the waterfront created problems for the city's MP. Montreal had an ocean outlet through a line to Portland in Maine, but many Canadians feared this dependence upon the United States and argued for an alternative line to Halifax. Unfortunately, the Maritime provinces were too poor to build major railways.

John A. Macdonald's finances were not much affected by the railway boom. He was associated with a scheme called the "Great Southern," which was never built. He bought land at Sarnia for a railway station, a controversial speculation which allegedly involved misuse of political influence. Instead, in 1856, he invested in a steamship, which promptly sank. Another aspect of Canada's steam revolution also impact negatively upon Macdonald. Steam-powered printing presses made possible Canada's first daily newspapers, and the *Globe* exploited Toronto's position as a rail hub to become Upper Canada's dominant journalistic force.

For the rest of his career, Macdonald faced a venomous opponent on his own patch.

Canada was also experiencing an administrative revolution, with bureaucratic reforms setting the foundations for today's federal civil service. In 1855, Macdonald appointed Canada's first auditor general, to impose discipline on government spending, while deputy ministers and entry tests were introduced in 1857. However, even routine matters still crossed ministerial desks, and all business was transacted longhand. Macdonald often complained he was "overwhelmed with work," "working like a beaver." When Parliament was sitting, his presence was required in the House at all hours. Campbell imagined his former partner keeping supporters in line with combinations of champagne and jokes "*of doubtful moral tendency.*" Macdonald was the only minister to serve throughout the eight years the coalition lasted, and the workload took an enormous toll.

Macdonald quickly carried legislation abolishing the clergy reserves, declaring it was "a great mistake in politics ... to resist when resistance is hopeless." However, he turned the tables on the Grits by granting the churches a favourable good deal. Britain insisted on safeguarding those clergy already receiving incomes from the reserves. Macdonald proposed to commute these payments, offering sixteen years' payment as a lump sum. However, he refused to buy out individual clerics, dealing instead with the churches that employed them. Far from depriving the Anglicans of State support, as Grits demanded, Macdonald handed them almost one million dollars, while the Presbyterians netted over $400,000 — permanent cash endowments replacing an unpopular land fund. He had captured the opposition's policy, and turned it inside out. If anything, the dodge was too clever. When Macdonald backed Confederation a decade later, many suspected his sincerity.

In May 1855, late in the parliamentary session, Macdonald pulled another trick. A bill passed through Parliament extending the privileges of Catholic schools in Upper Canada. Many politicians from the upper province had already gone home, and the measure was passed by French Canadian votes against Protestant objections. Resenting Lower Canadian interference in their local affairs, the Grits stepped up their demands for rep. by pop., a campaign that placed the two sections on a potential collision course.

Soon afterwards, the alternation of the capital back to Toronto enabled Macdonald to reunite his family, moving his wife and son from Kingston. The upheaval was too much for Isabella. In January 1856 she was so desperately ill that her new Toronto doctor warned she might die. Tory John Hillyard Cameron was Macdonald's party rival, but his wife stepped in to become Hugh John's child-minder. Coupled with his workload and money problems, Macdonald found his family crisis too much to bear. He had always been fond of a drink, but now he developed a full-scale alcohol problem. Early in 1856, his secretary twice noted that Macdonald was on a "spree," binge drinking to escape his worries. Soon, his weakness became a political embarrassment.

Late on February 26, John A. Macdonald, obviously drunk, berated George Brown in the Assembly. Even hardened politicians were shocked by his virulent language as he branded Brown "a convicted liar" who had "falsified evidence" to the Penitentiary Commission. Pale with fury, Brown demanded an investigation to clear his name. The next day, Macdonald tried to explain away comments made "in the heat of the debate" although, lawyer-like, he would neither "admit nor deny" whatever he was alleged to have said. "I am carrying on a war against that scoundrel George Brown," he told Helen, but only his mother could believe he was winning. Macdonald escaped formal censure since the committee of enquiry was stacked in his favour, but he failed to prove his most serious charges. Brown's enmity was now implacable.

Fortunately, Macdonald won the regard of his new Hincksite allies. Indeed, they wanted him to replace Sir Allan MacNab. Although only fifty-eight, MacNab was immobilized by gout and seemed a relic of bygone days. In May 1856, the Hincksite ministers walked out of Cabinet. Macdonald was desperately torn: MacNab was his leader, but he needed those ex-Reformers to stop the Tories from recapturing the party. Reluctantly, he also resigned, forcing MacNab into retirement. The fallen premier ridiculed "progressive conservatives or liberal progressives or what they call it." Macdonald defended himself, pointing out that MacNab had largely discarded "the conservative element" in forming his coalition government. But Macdonald made no reply when an opposition member sarcastically asked "whether, in future, he will call himself a Conservative or a Reformer?" John A. Macdonald emerged as Upper Canada leader in the reconstructed Cabinet, but at the cost of seeming devious and disloyal.

The alternating capital system, moving the administrative machine every four years, made no sense. Unfortunately, the Assembly could not agree on a permanent seat of government. Party discipline vanished, members voted for their local city and then combined to block more distant alternatives. In March 1857, the government decided to dodge the issue by referring the issue to Queen Victoria. The governor general, Sir Edmund Head, sent three-point secret advice to London: accept the request; delay the reply until after the next election; choose Ottawa. It proved a time bomb for Macdonald.

In July 1857, Macdonald made his third visit to Britain, his first as part of a government delegation. Isabella was "tolerably well" after her health crisis of the previous year: his secretary found her "very talkative." Indeed, in March 1857, she seemed in "very unusual health and strength." John A. Macdonald would not have crossed the ocean had there been a serious risk that he might return to find his wife dead and buried. Indeed, Isabella was well enough for her husband to plan on taking her on a New England vacation before escorting her to Kingston. There she would stay during the forthcoming elections, returning to Toronto when the new Assembly met.

The delegation to London failed to interest the British government in a railway linking Quebec with Halifax, but the visit to London gave Macdonald a valuable opportunity to think about British North America in a broader perspective. There were confidential discussions about the Hudson's Bay Company. Its trading monopoly west of the lakes would lapse in 1859, and the tacit assumption was that Canada would eventually inherit the prairies. A Nova Scotian delegation was also pressing for the Halifax-Quebec railway, and its leader, Premier James W. Johnston, favoured British North American union. Johnston probably persuaded Macdonald that Confederation would provide the framework to resolve Canada's internal divisions and support westward expansion — and that Nova Scotia would willingly join. But it was still an idea to be handled cautiously in Canada. The *Globe* exploded when it discovered from a Nova Scotian report that the delegates to Britain had discussed "a *Union of the British North American Provinces!* Who authorized Mr. Macdonald, in the name of ... the people of Canada, to proceed on such an embassy?"

"I am ... in good health and spirits & enjoying myself amazingly," Macdonald reported from England. He visited relatives, attended the opera, and when he became "tired of London," dashed over to Paris. Early in September, he returned to Canada, bearing luxury gifts for Isabella and a child's kilt to remind Hugh John of his Scottish heritage — and prepared to fight his fifth general election. Although ministries in the province of Canada were named after both sectional leaders, one co-premier was always the senior figure: Macdonald was the junior partner in the Taché-Macdonald Cabinet. With elections approaching, the respected Étienne Taché decided to bow out. He remained in the upper house, but George-Étienne Cartier, a combative Montrealer, succeeded him as Lower Canada leader. John A. Macdonald led the new Macdonald-Cartier Cabinet. On November 26, 1857, he became — in the grandiloquent terminology of a Kingston newspaper — "Prime Minister of Canada." At forty-two, Macdonald had achieved the highest office in his adopted country. It was the start of a nine-month nightmare that almost torpedoed his political career.

The new premier took over a tired ministry that had run out of ideas. He called an immediate election and, lacking eye-catching new policies, decided to campaign on the government's record. By contrast, Reformers energetically denounced Catholic schools and demanded representation by population. Many Conservatives felt pressured to agree that Upper Canada should have a larger say in running the province. Macdonald cynically advised one supporter to couple the issue with "extent of territory," to give country districts a counterweight against Toronto and Montreal. Farmers should be warned that urban politicians would tax them for big city projects. "These are good bunkum arguments." He also claimed that George Brown could never deliver representation by population, since he could only form a ministry if he found Lower Canadian allies, who would veto his plans. But Macdonald's specious arguments could not resist what he called the "fanatical" Protestant campaign.

Until 1874, general elections were spread over several weeks. As premier, Macdonald chose the order in which ridings polled, and he planned to raise his supporters' morale by beginning with his own return by acclamation at Kingston. He was "much disgusted" when a rival candidate spoiled his walkover. Although dismissed by Macdonald as a "fool," John Shaw was a local businessman and prominent member of the Orange Order. Shaw condemned Macdonald for failing to force the Grand Trunk to bring its line to Kingston's waterfront "before granting the aid they supplicated for." Of course, Macdonald could not hold a major provincial project to ransom for the benefit of his own riding, but Shaw's criticism illustrated the problems of combining advocacy of Kingston's interests with his responsibilities as provincial leader. Macdonald had in fact gifted the city three imposing public buildings, pushing them forward in 1855 "as in this uncertain world, no one can say, how long we are to last." His supporters failed to realize that heading a coalition of hungry supporters probably reduced his scope to direct resources to Kingston: one local newspaper wrote that as "Prime Minister," Macdonald's "power to do the city further good is almost illimitable." On December 17, 1857, he was re-elected by a massive 1,189 votes to nine, but his triumph was a high tide, not a benchmark, and disillusionment soon followed.

The Kingston victory was also an exception. Across Upper Canada, especially west of Toronto, government candidates were swept away by Grit demands for rep. by pop. and denunciations of Catholic schools. Bizarrely, two of Macdonald's colleagues, both prominent Orangemen, were defeated after being denounced as tools of the Pope. Nor did he lead a united team. "We are losing every where from our friends splitting the party," he complained. But there was no "party." His ministry was a coalition, formed *after* the previous elections. In Cabinet, Macdonald worked well with Reformers, but they had not created an integrated grass-roots organization and so, in the localities, rival candidates came forward. Every split "discourages our friends and strengthens our foes." Macdonald issued appeals for unity, hinting at future rewards for those who withdrew. He tried to coordinate the campaign from Toronto. "I cannot leave the helm here for a moment," he wrote, "or everything will go to the devil." Shaw's intervention forced him to spend a few days canvassing in Kingston, but he quickly returned to his headquarters. But on December 23, bad news made him hurry home again.

His mother had suffered a series of strokes in recent years, but this time Helen was likely felled by a virus, perhaps midwinter influenza: young Hugh John was also "seriously ill." Both recovered but, on December 28, Macdonald's wife Isabella died. She was forty-eight, and they had been married for fourteen years. Her life had often seemed precarious but her death was still unexpected. For a politician leading an election campaign, the bereavement was devastating. Political controversy was forgotten, wrote a Kingston journalist as he pictured Macdonald "sorrowing at his desolate fireside." (In fact, he was at his mother's house. His Brock Street residence had burned in 1856, and he never owned a Kingston home again.) A three-kilometre procession followed Isabella's coffin on December 30, the largest funeral in the city's history. But politics could not be forgotten, nor was sympathy universal. The *Globe* did not report Macdonald's bereavement, even unleashing a virulent attack on him on the morning of Isabella's burial. By January 3, 1858, Macdonald was back in Toronto, and his secretary thought him "pretty well under the circumstances." He had a government to run, and elections still to fight.

Although the Upper Canada results were bad, Macdonald's Lower Canada allies, the Bleus, swept to victory: the ministry would have a massive thirty-six seat overall majority in the Assembly. The shattered premier talked of resigning, but Sir Edmund Head persuaded him to continue. With three of his Cabinet colleagues defeated, his first task was to rebuild the Upper Canada section of the ministry, but how? "What to do I do not know," he wrote despairingly on January 16.

One possible avenue was to seek an alliance with George Brown's rival for the leadership of the Upper Canada Reformers, his near namesake, John Sandfield Macdonald. An attractive if sometimes abrasive character, "Sandfield" was bilingual, and a Catholic, although not especially devout (he once sued a priest for defamation after being likened to a mushroom on a dunghill). He opposed rep. by pop., which would weaken his political base in eastern Upper Canada by shifting power to the burgeoning districts further west. From Toronto, George Brown could defy the French, but Glengarry County and the tiny river port of Cornwall preferred a united Canada. "From Montreal we obtain our money," Sandfield explained. His fantasy solution to sectional confrontation was the "double majority": ministries must have strong support in both halves of the province. At intervals over the next decade, Macdonald would try to exploit the John A.–Sandfield–Brown triangle, seeking to use first one Reform leader and then the other, to checkmate his rival. But his first attempt failed. On January 26, Macdonald offered Sandfield two Cabinet seats, urging him to choose "a Reformer supporting the Government, *and not a Grit.*" A coded telegram, "All right," would signify agreement, but the reply was "No go." John A. Macdonald filled the vacant Cabinet posts from his own depleted ranks.

The 1858 parliamentary session was one of the longest and nastiest in Canadian history. Although the government's program contained little of importance, the Grits fought every inch of the way. By mid-March, John A. Macdonald was "hardly able to crawl" and privately he talked of finding a pretext to resign. "I find the work & annoyance too much for me." He needed space to grieve for Isabella, and perhaps he blamed himself for having left her in Kingston. He was drinking more than his exhausted system could handle. One evening in May, he delivered an alarmingly incoherent speech in Assembly. Soon after, it was announced that he had joined a temperance group, Macdonald himself admitting that "he had not been altogether free from blame in the course he pursued." The *Globe* called it "the funniest thing that has occurred for a long time." Canada's premier was becoming a figure of mockery.

One high-risk manoeuvre offered John A. Macdonald the chance to confound his tormenters. If his government could find an excuse to offer its resignation, his quarrelsome critics might find it difficult to unite, and impossible to secure an Assembly majority. Never having officially quit, Macdonald's colleagues could then bounce back stronger than before. It was an attractive tactic, for nobody believed that George Brown would find Lower Canada allies willing to make him premier: even Brown called himself a "government impossibility." Unfortunately for this dodge, Macdonald's solid French Canadian support gave him a bombproof majority. Only if he were defeated could there be a pretext to lure George Brown into the trap.

However, one issue threatened disunity among Macdonald's supporters. In January 1858, news arrived that Queen Victoria had chosen Ottawa as Canada's permanent capital. There was widespread protest against the selection of this primitive backwoods town: the *Globe* predicted that any public buildings erected in Ottawa would soon "be abandoned to the moles and the bats." Indeed, Premier Macdonald was in no hurry to start construction. "Do not say anything about any action of the Government on the matter," he warned the editor to whom he leaked the scoop. His Lower Canada supporters especially disliked the Queen's choice and, on July 28, a Bleu revolt carried a motion denouncing Ottawa by sixty-four votes to fifty. It was a parliamentary hiccup, but the next day, Macdonald tendered his Cabinet's resignation, in protest against the Assembly's "uncourteous insult" to the Queen. Since ministers had not snubbed their monarch, they had no reason to resign. Indeed, they had comfortably defeated a formal censure motion and so had no right to quit. The ensuing week of farcical intrigue damaged the reputation of public life, and branded John A. Macdonald as an inept trickster.

Still caretaker premier, Macdonald sat back to enjoy watching George Brown self-destruct in an impossible pursuit of power — in Macdonald's contemptuous image, like a greedy fish gobbling at the angler's bait. Unfortunately, Brown grabbed the bait and eluded the hook. Since Cabinets were small, there were only six Lower Canadian posts to fill, and the task proved unexpectedly easy. Antoine-Aimé Dorion was keen to show that his Rouges could tame the Toronto Protestant ogre, while Montreal's business community wanted its voice heard too. The Brown-Dorion ministry was sworn into office on August 2, and John A. Macdonald automatically became Canada's ex-premier. Worse still, the incoming team even offered some plausible policies. Disagreements over Catholic schools were mysteriously sidelined, but there was an important breakthrough on representation by population. Montreal Reformer Luther H. Holton encouraged Brown to consider restructuring the province as a two-headed (Ontario-Quebec) federation. Each section would run its own affairs, with Upper Canada having its rep. by pop. majority in the joint legislature. It looked a cumbersome constitution for just two million people: intriguingly, Brown wondered whether a union of all the provinces would make more sense. But the idea offered Lower Canadian politicians a device to protect their local interests while giving ground to Upper Canada's growing weight of numbers. The new ministry could also plead for time to work out the details. John A. Macdonald urgently needed to strangle the Brown-Dorion ministry in its cradle.

Macdonald was helped by the constitutional rule requiring ministerial by-elections. By accepting office, Brown's Cabinet colleagues ceased to be members of the Assembly until their ridings had re-endorsed them, further weakening their parliamentary numbers when attacked by Macdonald and Cartier. Ambush turned into massacre, with a censure motion passing by seventy-one votes to thirty-one. On his second day in office, Premier Brown asked the governor general to call an election. In a rare invocation of the Crown's prerogative, Sir Edmund Head refused. The governor general had already indicated that he might refuse to allow a fresh election but, as Head wrote privately, Brown believed "he could bully me into dissolving." Franchise qualifications had been relaxed in recent years, but no provision had been made for reliable voters' lists. During the recent elections, returning officers had been intimidated into accepting blatantly bogus claims: in Quebec City, thousands of dubious voters allegedly included British Prime Minister Lord Palmerston and French Emperor Napoleon III. Premier Macdonald had carried legislation to create voters' rolls, but these were not yet ready, and other abuses remained. Head argued that "a new election, under precisely the same laws, held within six to eight months of the last" would be equally unsatisfactory. However, Head was known to like Macdonald, and critics suspected a secret alliance between them. John A. himself angrily branded the charge of collusion "false as hell" but, in England, a senior civil servant suspected that Head was "too much under the influence of Macdonald." Frustrated and furious, Premier Brown resigned on August 4.

"Government no. 3 pretty much identical with no. 1," was Head's laconic summary of the outcome of a turbulent week. However, there was one notable change: the former ministers mostly returned, but Cartier was now premier. John A. Macdonald had been unlucky in his eight months at the provincial helm, politically in the lop-sided election result, personally through the hammer blow of Isabella's death. But politics is an unforgiving trade and, for all his efficiency, charm, and political cunning, John A. Macdonald had proved a disappointment in Canada's highest office. Worse still, he had formally admitted his alcohol problem. His resignation on a trumped-up pretext had proved a ludicrous miscalculation, although it would become a slow-burn grievance in Kingston that his premiership had made the rival city of Ottawa Canada's capital. Macdonald and Cartier remained allies but, down to 1867, the Montrealer was the senior partner. He was not pleased when Macdonald supplanted him as first prime minister of the Dominion.

The week of petty politicking played out in a bizarre finale. Somebody recalled that the law had been changed in 1857 to exempt ministers from fighting by-elections if they moved between portfolios within thirty days — a device to permit leisurely Cabinet reshuffles. Since Brown's "Short Administration" had survived only forty-eight hours, the returning ministers were well within the timeframe, so long as they accepted fresh portfolios. On August 6, John A. Macdonald was sworn in to Cartier's Cabinet as postmaster general. The next day, he resumed his old office as attorney general West. This was politics as a card game, and the episode was nicknamed the "double shuffle." Some said the ministers had accepted their joke jobs just before midnight, waited till the clock struck and then picked up their Bibles to swear themselves into their previous portfolios. Victorians were shocked at the sacrilege. Macdonald later implied that the dodge was not his idea but, for the remainder of his career, enemies remembered the squalid pantomime of the double shuffle.

Building Parliament in Canada's compromise capital Ottawa. His Kingston voters blamed Macdonald for backing the rival city.

Paradoxically, this shabby episode spawned an inspirational policy. Almost casually, the new ministry announced that it would ask the Maritime provinces to discuss how Confederation might "perhaps hereafter be practicable." The initiative was both tentative and tactical. It was the price paid for recruiting Alexander Galt, a reputed financial genius (although he had problems with the concept of a balanced budget) and an early enthusiast for British North American union. Cartier also needed a big idea to trump Grit talk of a two-headed Canadian federation, and Macdonald likely recalled Nova Scotian enthusiasm for the wider union in London the previous year. Above all, raising the Confederation issue might permit delay over Ottawa. Quebec City's campaign to become the permanent seat of government had argued that its central position between Canada and the Maritimes would make it the obvious capital of a united British North America. Discussing Confederation tacitly signalled to the Bleus that Ottawa might yet be dumped. However, the ploy was checkmated by the governor general's threat to resign unless Cartier backed the Queen's selection.

For Cartier's new ministry, the union of the provinces was more an aspiration, perhaps even just a slogan, than a practical policy. There was potential for disagreement over the design of any such union: would it imitate the American federation, in which Washington shared its authority with state legislatures, or copy Britain, where a single Parliament at Westminster ruled the entire United Kingdom? Cartier wanted French Canadians to control their own autonomous unit, but Macdonald admired the British constitution, a preference confirmed by the outbreak of the American Civil War in 1861. In 1858, this difference was papered over with the phrase "a bond of a federal character" — "bond" meant strong, "federal" meant weak. The initiative petered out in a round of dispatches and delegations, but the Confederation genie was out of the bottle, and the issue returned to the political agenda in 1864.

Macdonald's disappointing premiership left his career curiously becalmed at the very top of politics. He claimed he was "unwilling" to return to office in August 1858, "but Cartier would not do anything without me." His health was poor and, by November, it was "no secret" that he was planning to quit politics altogether. "Having been First Minister, he has no higher point to reach," wrote a friendly journalist. The Grits launched a private prosecution to challenge the legality of the double shuffle. Macdonald faced massive fines if he lost the case. In fact he won, but the action was launched in the name of a man who was bankrupt, so he could not recover his costs. The *Globe* alleged that the thought of losing Macdonald created panic among "the hungry, unprincipled crew who call him leader." But was he really indispensable? In July 1859, Macdonald discovered that Galt and Cartier had authorized a major bank guarantee without telling him. Angry that he had "*not been consulted*," he drafted a resignation letter. Maybe he never sent it: the risk of acceptance was too great. In fact, Macdonald was probably not consulted because he had been adrift on a steamboat in Georgian Bay. He had joined an inspection tour — a political junket — sailing to Sault Ste. Marie, but the ship's engines had failed and the helpless vessel drifted dangerously close to the rocky Bruce Peninsula. Even George Brown was shocked at how close Canada's political elite had come to perishing. "Little as I owe them, I would not like them to go off in that way." John A. Macdonald did not travel west again until 1886, when he rode the train to the Pacific.

Although there were further threats to quit in 1861 and 1862, Macdonald was remarkably tenacious in office. His "private affairs" were in such disarray that in November 1858, he appealed to an associate to be "a good fellow" and help him out of a "scrape" by hurrying a payment owed to him. John A. Macdonald picked his business associates badly. In August 1859, he arrived in Kingston to find his property seized for auction thanks to the default of a hard-up colleague whose finances he had recklessly underwritten. "I am quite unable to pay my own debts & meet this one of yours as well." One observer wondered how "a man of so much intellect and versatility" could be "such a child" about money. A partner in a Kingston real estate development complained in 1861, "Macdonald has all but ruined me by his wretched carelessness." Yet, despite his resolve in July 1862 to "set to work to make a little money," Macdonald remained addicted to politics.

Isabella's death had left him with sole responsibility for his son Hugh John. The Macdonald of the 1840s had delighted in playing with a young nephew, pretending to owe the little boy huge sums of money and emptying his pockets of coin to pay the imaginary debt. But the most popular politician in Canada now seemed too busy and remote to be a proper father to "Hughey." Parenting responsibilities fell upon his sister Margaret, who had married a Queen's academic, widower James Williamson. The childless Williamsons were "kind & judicious" in rearing the boy, and Macdonald's letters sent praise and kisses, but somehow his staccato correspondence conveyed little affection for Hugh and not overmuch appreciation for the help of his in-laws. Hugh Macdonald became an insecure adult.

Meanwhile, Macdonald's political career descended towards disaster. In 1860 Queen Victoria sent her son, the Prince of Wales (the future Edward VII), on the first royal tour of Canada, under the guardianship of the Duke of Newcastle, the British

Cabinet minister responsible for the colonies. Kingston was their first Upper Canadian port of call, and Macdonald planned a glittering ball at which his constituents could meet the prince. He was not alone in planning a welcome. Catholic priests had been prominent in civic ceremonies in French Canada, and Kingston's Orangemen determined to parade in their regalia under triumphal arches to demonstrate that Canada was a Protestant country too. Unfortunately, the Orange Order was banned in Ireland and the duke refused to countenance its existence. When the royal steamboat arrived at Kingston, a furious row broke out, with Macdonald insisting that the Order was a legal body in Canada, Newcastle refusing to allow the prince to land, and the Orangemen standing their ground on the waterfront. The gala ball was a flop, despite Macdonald's bogus claim that "His Royal Highness had expressed his sincere regret at the unfortunate misunderstanding." After a twenty-four-hour standoff, the prince sailed away. Macdonald had furiously told the duke that "if they passed Kingston by, they should also pass him by." For the next two weeks, the senior minister from Upper Canada boycotted the royal tour. The politician who had resigned because Parliament had insulted Queen Victoria over Ottawa had placed himself in the invidious position of snubbing her son and heir. Eventually, Macdonald swallowed his pride and rejoined the official party. Not surprisingly, there were suspicions he had been on drunken bender.

Macdonald's political standing was so shaken that he embarked on a speaking tour of the province, to rebuild his grassroots support. "I never took to the *stump* before," he commented, but he enjoyed the experience. Unfortunately, extremist Orangemen believed Macdonald had not done enough to defend them, and at the next elections, in the summer of 1861, his Protestant power base in Kingston was fractured. His one-time law pupil, Oliver Mowat, was imported from Toronto to run against him — it was no accident that Mowat was a prominent teetotaller. Kingston rejected the interloper by 785 votes to 484, a come-down from Macdonald's eleven hundred vote triumph in 1857. He owed his victory to Catholic voters, many of whom backed him as the lesser of two evils. Macdonald's majority was less secure than it appeared.

The Conservatives did well across Upper Canada but, para-doxically, success added to Macdonald's problems. To his puz-zlement, "the dry bones of Pre-Adamite Toryism" had stirred into new life. By abolishing the clergy reserves, he had done the extreme Tories the favour of freeing them from an unpopu-lar cause. The 1861 elections were held soon after preliminary results from that year's census showed that Upper Canada now had 1.4 million people, well ahead of Lower Canada's 1.1 million. Tories increasingly vented their contempt for French Catholics under the fair-play guise of demanding representation by population. Macdonald condemned the "violent Tories" who stupidly believed "that a purely Conservative Government can be formed." Any such attempt would merely reunite all brands of Reformers, who collectively had a built-in majority in go-ahead Upper Canada. "I am not such a fool as to destroy all that I have been doing for the last 7 years." But when Cabinet changes were needed in March 1862, it was impossible to find any Conservative opposed to rep. by pop. Indeed, the Tories demanded that they should dominate the government. An emerging Lower Canadian centre group, the Mauves (a mixture of Rouge and Bleu) added to the instability.

The outbreak of the American Civil War created fresh challenges. In November 1861 a Northern warship seized two Southern envoys travelling to Europe on a British steamship. Britain angrily demanded an apology, and war was briefly threatened. The crisis destroyed any lingering belief that the Empire could protect Canada from invasion. British reinforcements were rushed across the Atlantic, although the lack of a railway from Halifax prevented most from reaching the interior of Canada. The imperial garrison was boosted to 14,000 troops. This would have deterred the 16,000-strong pre-1861 United States Army, but it was useless against the massive forces engaged in the Civil War: the North suffered 15,000 casualties in a single week of battles in June 1862 — and went on fighting.

Nominally, every adult male from sixteen to fifty served in Canada's militia: that was why Macdonald had marched against Mackenzie's rebels in 1837. Now, as the first-ever minister of militia, he introduced a sweeping reform measure, to create a part-time army, intensively (and expensively) trained. The details of his Militia Bill were both vague and alarming. Military experts spoke of training 100,000 men; Macdonald talked of 50,000, maybe costing a million dollars. Financially, this was a nightmare: Galt's latest budget already planned to spend $12 million — but revenue would be only $7 million. If there were too few volunteers, conscription would make up the numbers, something especially unpopular in French Canada. Cartier seemed notably unenthusiastic about his own government's proposal, and Macdonald's handling of the measure was lacklustre. Worse still, some days the bill stalled because the minister did not appear in Parliament. Macdonald's absences were caused "nominally by illness," noted the new governor general, Lord Monck, "but really, as every one knows, by drunkenness." On May 20, 1862, a Bleu revolt defeated the Militia Bill, and Cartier's ministry resigned.

Calling defeat "a grateful tonic," Macdonald put his usual favourable spin on events. "I chose a soft bed to fall upon ... I fell in a blaze of loyalty." Perhaps a new phase was opening in his career. The death of Helen Macdonald in October 1862 freed him from acting out his mother's ambitions. Soon afterwards, he made a private visit to England on Trust and Loan Company business: maybe, at last, he could concentrate on making some money. Although claiming to be "thoroughly sick of official life," Macdonald still planned to exercise political influence, "to keep my place in parliament ... I can do more good there." But while he remained in politics, sheer ability made him an inescapable choice as party leader. Even in the aftermath of the Militia Bill debacle, the "immeasurably inferior" John Hillyard Cameron failed to oust him as caucus leader. As the governor of New Brunswick wrote in 1865, "Macdonald (when not drunk) is a really powerful man." Once again, John A. Macdonald dealt with the alcohol issue by announcing he would join the temperance movement.

The new premier, Sandfield Macdonald, skilfully kept his insecure ministry afloat for twenty-two months. Unfortunately, his big idea, the double majority, ensured that the divided province achieved little at a time when there were so many challenges to tackle. John A. Macdonald even put out feelers for a possible alliance with George Brown. Brown replied that he would "sustain" a Conservative ministry if it enacted representation by population. However, he rejected coalition as "demoralizing" and refused "friendly personal intercourse" with Macdonald until his 1856 allegations were "entirely withdrawn."

John A. Macdonald promised to provide "gentlemanlike and patriotic opposition" in Parliament. Sandfield's ministry was "in a great mess & cannot possibly go on, but I am doing what I can to keep them up," he claimed in March 1863. "They will fall from their own weakness and not from the attacks of the opposition." Six weeks later, as mighty American armies clashed at Chancellorsville, he carried a censure motion and forced Sandfield into a general election: continental crisis had not yet compelled Canada's politicians to soar above faction fighting. Campaigning as "a simple citizen of Kingston," Macdonald faced Reformer Overton S. Gildersleeve, a young, respected, and highly successful local businessman. Gildersleeve's vote equalled Mowat's 1861 tally, marking him as a long-term threat. The Conservatives did badly across Upper Canada but the overall political situation remained unstable. Sandfield clung to a wafer-thin majority but, on March 21, 1864, he staged a tactical resignation, boasting that his opponents could not replace him.

At first, John A. Macdonald refused to accept office: he had "strong private reasons urging him to look more closely to his own affairs." Once again, the wild card of mortality had intervened. Although only forty-one, his partner, Archie John MacDonell, was fatally ill: his death, on March 27, automatically dissolved their law firm. Winding up their joint accounts would reveal that the practice was chronically insolvent. "It was utter ruin to me to return to the Government and I declined," Macdonald later recalled. Taking office would also mean fighting a ministerial by-election, and Macdonald had probably concluded months earlier that the ambitious Gildersleeve would throw money into such a contest which the near-bankrupt John A. could not match. But death took a hand here too. On March 9, aged just thirty-nine, Gildersleeve died of a heart attack. Kingston's Reformers had no obvious alternative candidate, and John A. Macdonald might survive a by-election after all.

Premier Sandfield Macdonald was indeed hard to replace. A Reformer, A.J. Fergusson-Blair, failed to form a ministry,

Cartier ran into problems, and there was even talk of drafting Alexander Campbell, who had never held office. Étienne Taché was prepared to come out of retirement, but he demanded John A. Macdonald as his Upper Canada deputy. Macdonald was "wrapped in slumber" late one March evening when Cartier, Campbell, and Fergusson-Blair hammered at the front door of his lodgings and roused him from his midnight slumber. They delivered an ultimatum. If he would not forget his business worries and join them, they would abandon their attempts to form a Cabinet and allow Sandfield to bounce back in triumph. John A. Macdonald did not need long to consider. He returned to the dreary wasteland of colonial politics.

4

1864–1867
Confederation, Under a Female Sovereign

The insecure government formed by Etienne Taché in March 1864 faced collapse within eleven weeks. Nonetheless, John A. Macdonald's decision to take office under Taché proved a turning point in his career. In mid-June, the Cabinet was reconstructed to become the "Great Coalition" which launched Confederation. The revised ministry was essentially a deal between Cartier's Bleus and George Brown's Grits: if Macdonald had not already joined in March, there would have been no room to bring him aboard in June.

Aside from its collective desire to oust Sandfield Macdonald, the March 1864 minority government had no "big idea." Sandfield had quarrelled with the Irish Catholics, so their representative, Reformer Michael Foley, was invited into the new Cabinet. When Foley cautiously enquired about the ministry's guiding principles, John A. Macdonald jovially urged him to "join the Government and then help make the policy." In Parliament, Macdonald implied that the new Cabinet endorsed the Confederation bid of 1858. "The Government had done all in its power to have this federation remedy adopted" — but, unfortunately, the Maritimers were not interested. As a policy statement, it was watertight. As a blueprint for action, it was unhelpful.

Taking an independent line in politics, Brown secured a parliamentary committee on constitutional change. His task force reported in June "in favour of changes in the direction of a federative system" — but whether for the province of Canada or the whole of British North America remained an open question. John A. Macdonald opposed the report: he favoured "a complete union," but he knew compromise was required. His 1861 election manifesto had briefly talked of federation, but with "an efficient central government" — the British model adapted to learn from American failures. The mid-June ministerial crisis concluded with George Brown joining the Cabinet to resolve Canada's sectional disagreements. Although it united to carry Confederation, the Great Coalition was also a continuation of factional fighting in a new guise: Brown and Macdonald grasped each other not by the hand but by the throat. In the tense negotiations of June 1864, Macdonald out-manoeuvred his enemy on four issues, but — on the most crucial — his victory contained a time bomb.

As in 1862, Brown initially promised independent support for constitutional reform, claiming it was "quite impossible" for him to sit in Cabinet alongside political enemies. It was easy to foresee that some issue would soon outrage Brown's implacable conscience, and Macdonald was not alone in insisting that it was "essential" that he joined. Macdonald then faced down Brown's reasonable demand that the Grits, dominant in Upper Canada, should have four of that section's six Cabinet places: his rival conceded only three. Macdonald's comment that "he had been for some time, anxious to retire from the Government, and would be quite ready to facilitate arrangements by doing so," was a threatening reminder that he was indispensable. A third issue was Brown's demand that Macdonald publicly retract the allegations he had made between 1849 and 1856 over the penitentiary enquiry. It seems that Macdonald soothingly sidestepped the commitment. Brown never received his "public reparation," and his resentment festered at being cheated of revenge.

The fourth — and major — issue concerned the coalition's policy. Brown wanted to reorganize the province of Canada as a local (Ontario-Quebec) federation, with provision for the Maritimes and the West to join later. Initially, of course, the central legislature would be dominated by Upper Canada's population and hence run by Upper Canada's Grits — a structure that might be unattractive to potential new members. Macdonald's counter-proposal, "a Federal Union of all the British North American Provinces," was dismissed by Brown as "uncertain and remote," no solution to the "existing evils." However, one development worked in favour of the wider scheme. The governments of New Brunswick, Nova Scotia, and Prince Edward Island were considering an Atlantic regional union. *If* the Canadians could secure an invitation to the planned Maritime Union conference in September, and *if* they could argue persuasively for Confederation, then the larger union might become a practical option. "If it had not been for this fortunate coincidence of events," Macdonald said in 1865, "never, perhaps ... would we have been able to bring this scheme to a practical conclusion." The Great Coalition struck a deal. Ministers would "address themselves, in the most earnest manner, to the negotiation for a confederation of all the British North American Provinces." But, if the initiative failed, they would legislate "in the next session of Parliament" to create a local federation for Canada alone.

Given parliamentary timetables, Macdonald had gained maybe nine months to launch the dormant project of Confederation before conceding victory to Brown. His best hope was to play for time and extend the deadline. But everything depended upon winning over a group of small-pond Maritime politicians, most of them strangers to him. If they said "No" at Charlottetown, John A. Macdonald's career would hit the buffers. Working hard to prepare an outline scheme, and with his business affairs in disarray, he was under great pressure that summer, even appearing at one Cabinet meeting aggressively drunk.

Fortunately, despite much champagne diplomacy, he remained sober and performed impressively at Charlottetown. Although the meetings were held in secret, we know that the Canadians — Brown, Galt, and Cartier included — swept their hosts into endorsing Confederation in principle. The delegates then sailed on to Halifax where, on September 12, John A. Macdonald delivered a heartfelt speech. He had spent "twenty long years" dragging himself through "the dreary waste" of provincial politics. "I thought there was no end, nothing worthy of ambition" but Confederation was "well worthy of all I have suffered in the cause of my little country." He accepted that that "local difficulties may arise ... local jealousies may intervene" but asserted that the union of the provinces was "a fixed fact." "Union must take place some time. I say now is the time." On the return journey, the delegates visited New Brunswick to speak at Saint John. It was a worrying sign that Macdonald was too exhausted to leave the ship.

On October 10, 1864, provincial delegations began a three-week conference at Quebec to convert the outline agreement of Charlottetown into a constitutional blueprint. "Unless the details can be made satisfactory the whole thing must break down,"

Macdonald warned. He called for "a powerful central government," with the provinces assigned "only such powers as may be required for local purposes." He reminded the Maritimers of the coalition's timetable, warning that if Canada was compelled to tackle its own problems, "it will be too late for a general federation." He also told them that the "Intercolonial" railway from Halifax to Quebec was conditional on Confederation, "a political consequence of a political union."

D'Arcy McGee later claimed that John A. Macdonald crafted fifty of the seventy-two resolutions that comprised the Quebec scheme. "Not one man of the Conference (except Galt on finance) had the slightest idea of Constitution making," Macdonald privately boasted. "Whatever is good or ill in the constitution is mine." Would there have been a Confederation movement without John A. Macdonald? Probably. Would it have been led with the same skill and efficiency? Perhaps not.

Macdonald was open about his belief that "one government and one parliament ... would be the best, the cheapest, the most vigorous and the strongest system of government we could adopt." Realistically, he also recognized that centralization was unacceptable to French Canadians, because they were "a minority, with a different language, nationality, and religion." But a "smoking gun" in a letter to Tory politician, Matthew Crooks Cameron, might suggest he was playing a secret double game. Cameron admitted that the "federal principle does not inspire me with a feeling of confidence," but John A. Macdonald reassured him that "we have hit upon the only practicable plan — I do not say the best plan ... for carrying out the Confederation." He went further, predicting that British North America would evolve into a unitary state: "you, if spared the ordinary age of men, will see both Local Parliaments & Governments absorbed in the General power. This is as plain to me as if I saw it accomplished but of course it does not do to adopt that point of view in discussing the subject in Lower Canada." Was there was a deep-laid plot to smuggle some toxic provision into the constitution, a poison time-capsule that the forty-two-year-old Cameron would live to see destroy the provinces? Hardly. Macdonald was trying to hoodwink Cameron with "spin," and even that failed. When Cameron argued for a legislative union in Parliament, Macdonald replied that French Canadians and Maritimers opposed a unitary scheme. "How, then, is it to be accomplished?" Macdonald knew that Cameron was a gentleman, and gentlemen did not divulge private correspondence.

Indeed, Macdonald rejected the best instrument for destroying the provinces. The Fathers of Confederation used New Zealand's federal constitution as a quarry: it was even the source of the celebrated phrase "peace, order and good government." That document gave the colony's General Assembly power to abolish New Zealand's constituent provinces, which it exercised in 1876. But when the Nova Scotian centralizer Jonathan McCully argued for copying this provision, Macdonald retorted: "That is just what we do not want." John A. Macdonald did not plot to undermine Canada's provinces.

The workload of the Quebec Conference took its toll. "John A. Macdonald is always drunk now," commented one observer: he was found in his hotel room, a rug draped over his nightshirt, in front of a mirror declaiming Hamlet. The genial "John A." was in overdrive, designing Canada's new constitution at the expense of his own. After the conference, the delegates headed for a banquet in the nearly-complete Ottawa Parliament Buildings. Keynote speaker would be John A. Macdonald, "but illness ... compelled him to curtail his observations." Two weeks later he was "still weak." "I got a severe shock at Ottawa and was very near going off the books," he admitted. Although his collapse was reportedly "induced by fatigue from assiduous attention to public affairs," alcohol was a rumoured contributory cause. However, six years later, Macdonald was diagnosed as suffering from gallstones. His 1864 illness perhaps resulted from the banqueting that accompanied the Quebec Conference, too much rich food for his tender gallbladder.

While he was designing a new constitution, Macdonald was also running the existing government machine — and a time of continental crisis as the American Civil War moved to a close. Southern sympathizers marooned in Canada were arrested after raiding a bank in the border town of St. Albans, Vermont. In mid-December, 1864, C.J. Coursol, a lowly Montreal magistrate, freed them on a technicality, and the raiders even recovered their loot. Macdonald hoped to escape Quebec to spend Christmas in Kingston, "but if there are other such fools as Coursol in the world, I'll never get away." He established Canada's first secret service, to collect intelligence on Southern sympathizers, and also to watch a new menace, the Fenians, an American-based paramilitary organization that aimed to free Ireland by attacking Canada.

In February 1865, the Canadian Parliament debated Confederation, with Macdonald leading off for the government. Unusually, he had rehearsed his speech. Indeed, his Quebec City landlord feared for Macdonald's sanity when his distinguished tenant locked himself in his room and harangued the lodging-house cat. Even so, it was a low-key performance. Speaking for several hours, Macdonald outlined the unexciting details of the proposed structure, insisting that the Quebec scheme was a "treaty" agreed with the Maritimers, a package that Canada's legislators must not amend. Calling Confederation "an opportunity that may never recur," he concluded by hailing "the happy opportunity now offered of founding a great nation." Calling it "the feeblest speech he had ever delivered," Reformer Luther Holton claimed that the centralist Macdonald did not truly believe in the federal system he had helped devise. The charge rankled, and weeks into the marathon debate Macdonald delivered a sparkling extempore rebuttal: maybe his earlier speech had sounded feeble, "but as to my sentiments on Confederation, they were the sentiments of my life, my sentiments in Parliament years ago, my sentiments in the Conference, and my sentiments now."

Macdonald's speech was downbeat partly because it was the curtain-raiser to a comprehensive ministerial battery: Galt talked about finance, Brown and Cartier the advantages of Confederation to Upper and Lower Canada, while D'Arcy McGee supplied the oratorical fireworks. Another factor was disturbing news from the Maritimes, where public opinion was startled by the novelty of the project. Indeed, in New Brunswick, Premier Tilley had already been forced to call an election, rather than face a mutinous local Assembly. Overheated speeches in the Canadian Assembly might sound suspiciously triumphal on the Atlantic seaboard. Indeed, Macdonald unwittingly created problems for his Maritime allies by stating that the promised Intercolonial Railway would not form "a portion of the Constitution." Tilley's opponents jumped on the statement, claiming that the Canadians could not be trusted.

The news, early in March, that New Brunswickers had in fact voted against Confederation showed John A. Macdonald at his fighting best. He frankly accepted that Tilley's election defeat was "a declaration against the policy of Federation," but he roundly refused to abandon the cause. Rather, the setback was "an additional reason for prompt and vigorous action." The New

Brunswick reverse, "the first check that the project has received," only highlighted the astonishing progress the issue had made since the formation of the coalition in June 1864.

"Things are not going on so badly with the Maritime Provinces," he wrote optimistically. "In New Brunswick the question will ere long be carried. Nova Scotia is all right but hangs fire until New Brunswick is put straight." In fact, this analysis reflected something more than Macdonald's habitual tendency to put a positive spin on bad news. The New Brunswick result was closer than the landslide in seats suggested: several pro-Confederation candidates had only narrowly lost. In any case, the contest had been "the usual fight between the ins and the outs," with "a lot of other influences at work" besides the Confederation issue. Although the new ministry was united in opposing the Quebec scheme, their reasons were contradictory: some opposed any union with Canada, others criticized the terms. Macdonald was right about Nova Scotia too. Premier Charles Tupper, with whom he had struck a rapport at Charlottetown, was masterfully controlling the local political agenda, keeping Confederation on the backburner to avoid its outright rejection. If Canada kept up the momentum, the New Brunswick ministry might well break up. The big prize for the Maritimers in Confederation was the Intercolonial Railway. Once New Brunswick changed sides, Nova Scotia would fall into line to ensure that Halifax and not Saint John became its Atlantic terminus. In April 1865, Tupper reckoned the situation could be turned around in twelve months.

Unfortunately, Macdonald did not have twelve months. The June 1864 coalition deal committed ministers to George Brown's plan for a federation of the two Canadas if the wider union was not achieved by mid-1865. Dispatched to England in November 1864 to report on the Quebec Conference, George Brown had been hailed by Britain's statesmen as the messenger of Confederation. Privately, however, he was relaxed about the setback in New Brunswick, and ready to insist on his Plan B. Macdonald announced that a delegation would be sent to London, to mobilize imperial support for Confederation. Brown had to be persuaded to make a second transatlantic trip within six months — getting him on board ship was crucial to keeping him on board politically. Accordingly, the delegation's agenda was extended to include cross-border trade and the future of the Hudson's Bay territories, both issues of concern to Brown. Cartier and Galt represented Lower Canada and Macdonald, despite a reluctance to travel, would speak for Upper Canada. Brown could not trust his rivals to represent Canada's interests; they could not risk leaving him behind, where he might find some pretext to break up the coalition. So, in April 1865, Brown crossed the ocean once again, travelling with John A. Macdonald. Indeed, in the confined shipboard space, the two men had to pretend they were friends as well as allies.

The Canadian mission to Britain made a mighty splash, and the delegates received a welcome unprecedented for mere colonials. Famous statesmen engaged them in top-level conferences. They were presented to Queen Victoria, entertained by the Prince of Wales and given a memorable excursion to England's famous horse race, the Derby. However, British politicians limited their support to polite goodwill. They were wary about spending money on defending Canada against the Americans, and seemed to view Confederation as a step towards transatlantic disengagement. The delegation's major achievement, as Macdonald put it, was that they "happily succeeded in keeping the question alive" in Britain. The British government issued a strong declaration of support for Confederation, enough to ward off immediate pressure to restructure the province of Canada alone. For Macdonald, there was also a personal prize: Oxford University awarded him an honorary doctorate. Oxford ceremonies could be raucous, but "Mr. Macdonald, the Canadian, had a good reception." To be announced back at Government House as "Dr. Macdonald" offered some consolation for the inadequacy of his own education: Gowan thought that the Oxford degree "would gratify you more than a knighthood." Macdonald modestly accepted the honour on behalf of Canada, but it was noteworthy that he was singled out as the recipient.

Soon after Macdonald's return to Canada, there was a sharp, sad reminder of the tight agenda facing the coalition. Premier Taché had sacrificed his health in launching the new Canada, and died on July 30, 1865. An incandescent George Brown blocked Lord Monck's attempt to appoint John A. Macdonald as Taché's successor. Brown's price for accepting the Quebec City lawyer Sir Narcisse-Fortunat Belleau (a member of Macdonald's 1857–58 Cabinet) as compromise premier was the re-statement of the coalition's dual objective, reaffirming the commitment to create a purely Canadian federation if the wider project stalled. The deadline was shifted back to 1866.

With Belleau a figurehead, Macdonald effectively led the government. Paradoxically, political leadership involved keeping the lid on Canadian politics to avoid rows that might inflame Maritime suspicions. Upper and Lower Canada would enter Confederation as separate provinces (named Ontario and Quebec in 1867) but Canadians were left to perform their own bisection. Discussion of the new provincial constitutions would certainly reignite controversy over Catholic schools. Since the Irish Catholic vote was important in New Brunswick, Macdonald simply delayed the 1866 session of Canada's legislature. New Brunswick politicians insisted that they favoured uniting the provinces but disliked the Quebec Conference terms — but Canada's Parliament had signed up to the Quebec package. As Macdonald explained, once Canada's legislature met, ministers would be "pressed to declare whether we adhered to the Quebec resolutions or not." To answer "yes" would condemn his New Brunswick allies to defeat, but "no" would outrage French Canada: either way would be "good-bye to Federation." In his later career, Macdonald would be nicknamed "Old Tomorrow." In the winter of 1865–66, he first showed his skills at procrastination.

Throughout the winter of 1865–66, reports from New Brunswick confidently predicted the slow-motion disintegration of opposition to Confederation. Tilley became premier again in April 1866, and in a June election he won a pro-Union election majority — helped by campaign funds quietly raised among Macdonald's Canadian supporters. Meanwhile, in December 1865, George Brown resigned from the coalition, ostensibly over the handling of trade talks in Washington: characteristically, if unrealistically, Brown had argued that the provinces should stand up to the Americans and force them to renew the cross-border Reciprocity Treaty. Cartier and Campbell tried to persuade Brown not to quit, but for Macdonald, the parting was a relief, the more so as the other Reformers in the coalition preferred working with John A. to taking orders from George Brown. However, Brown's resignation meant that the *Globe* could resume its vendetta against Macdonald. It was not long before John A. Macdonald supplied the pretext.

Symbolic of the approaching new era, Canada's capital finally moved to Ottawa. Macdonald founded the elite Rideau Club to provide social amenities, but the city's general lack of facilities — ominously, Ottawa lacked even a piped water supply — had what Lord Monck discreetly called "a damaging effect on public men." Despite the fiasco of 1862, Macdonald was once again minister of militia, and bearing a heavy responsibility. With the end of the Civil War, Irish-American soldiers joined the Fenians who planned to attack Canada. Mobilizing Canada's defence forces every time there was an invasion alarm would paralyze the provincial economy, but failure to respond to a credible warning would risk Canadian lives. Macdonald struck the right balance: 14,000 part-time soldiers were called out on May 31, the day nine hundred Fenians crossed the Niagara River. Two days later, the paramilitaries killed nine militiamen at the Battle of Ridgeway. The invaders withdrew and the American authorities belatedly tightened up border security, but the threat remained. Macdonald dismissed calls for the summary arrest of suspected Fenian sympathizers: "illiterate magistrates" would simply persecute their peaceable Catholic neighbours. It was difficult to persuade the public that the government was on top of the danger. "Because they do not see what we are doing in the Newspapers, they think we are doing nothing."

The delay caused by New Brunswick was not the only constraint on the Confederation timetable. By the time Canada's legislature finally met in June 1866, the governor general was "uneasy." Britain's Parliament generally took a holiday between August and February, but in 1866 an autumn session seemed likely to tackle a political crisis over parliamentary reform. Lord Monck wanted to complete Canada's preparations, travel to London, and pass the Confederation act before the close of 1866. On June 21, he threatened to resign if Confederation faltered. Macdonald read the governor general a polite lecture on constitutional responsibility, urging Monck to trust "my Canadian Parliamentary experience." As for Confederation, "success is certain, and it is now not even a question of strategy. It is merely one of tactics." But uncertainty returned when Britain's Liberal government resigned and an inexperienced minority Conservative ministry took office. There would be no autumn session, and if the parliamentary reform issue could not be resolved when Westminster reassembled early in 1867, a British general election would follow. Nova Scotians were due to vote too, around June 1867. Although the colony's politicians had fallen into line with New Brunswick, proud Bluenoses might well reject Confederation.

Drafting legislation would require "weeks of anxious and constant labour" in England, but preparations seemed lethargic in Ottawa. Proposed local constitutions for Upper and Lower Canada were introduced on July 13, 1866, but there was no sense of urgency about ratifying them. On August 6, the *Globe* denounced the delay as "shameful," ominously blaming "Ministerial incapacity." It was "the common talk of Ottawa" that Macdonald was responding to pressure in his usual deplorably liquid way: Monck's resignation threat had likely been a coded warning. In mid-August, the *Globe* abandoned all restraint to report that Macdonald had made a "wild and incoherent" speech in Parliament, proof that he was "in a state of gross intoxication." George Brown's newspaper broadened its attack over a three-week period. Never before, it claimed, had a Cabinet minister been "seen to hold on to his desk to prevent himself from falling ... with utterance so thick as to be almost incomprehensible ... so utterly gone at mid-day as to be unconscious of what he was doing." Macdonald's drunken bouts threatened the "postponement of Confederation."

Macdonald's alcohol problem was no secret, but public attitudes to drink were ambivalent. One supporter even urged him "not to rely on Cold Water, & tea, & coffee *alone*, to sustain your not very robust &, sometimes over-wrought frame." Macdonald had twice publicly admitted his need to reform, but the temperance groups he joined were widely viewed as cranks and killjoys. Macdonald often joked about his weakness, claiming that Canadians preferred John A. drunk to George Brown sober. Legend claimed that Macdonald once shocked an audience by vomiting during a public debate, but charmed them by explaining that his opponent's policies turned his stomach. Pressures of the Confederation timetable plus his lonely Ottawa existence probably explain why Macdonald was drinking heavily. Friendship with fellow minister D'Arcy McGee, another notorious boozer, worsened the problem. The *Globe* declared that "never before were two Ministers of the Crown seen at one time rolling helplessly on the Ministerial bench." Legend claimed that Macdonald told his colleague that the Cabinet could not afford two drunks — so McGee must give up alcohol. Macdonald threatened to sue, but the case never came to court, and even his apologists did not deny the stories. Instead, his defenders organized a banquet in his honour, held at Kingston on September 5, where the impressively sober guest of honour obliquely deplored the "wanton and unprovoked attack" upon him. Guest speakers lavished generous praise as damage limitation, but one speech was so exaggerated it almost destroyed Macdonald's career.

Leading an anti-Confederation delegation in London, the veteran Nova Scotian politician Joseph Howe pounced upon McGee's overblown statement that Macdonald had crafted fifty of the seventy-two Quebec resolutions. On October 3, Howe released a statement "charitably" attributing the "incoherent" nature of the Confederation project to alcoholic excess, and asking why Maritimers should be ruled by Canadian politicians who "cannot govern themselves." Alarm bells rang at the highest levels of the Empire. The *Globe* had specifically charged that Macdonald had been drunk during the Fenian raid, and Lord Monck had privately confirmed that the minister of militia had been "incapable of all official business for days on end." London bureaucrats were aghast at Macdonald's behaviour. One argued that they should "endeavour to get the Offender ousted." Senior civil servant Frederic Rogers hoped "the Canadians will have the good sense to keep Mr. John A. Macdonald on the other side of the Atlantic." There were urgent consultations among British Cabinet ministers. The colonial secretary, Lord Carnarvon, concluded that "in spite of his notorious vice," Macdonald was "the ablest politician in Upper Canada." Losing Macdonald "would absolutely destroy Confederation"; without Confederation, Canada would eventually join the United States. In a carefully worded letter to Monck, sent on October 19, Carnarvon avoided naming the offender but stressed that "undoubted ability" was no excuse for drunkenness. By the time he sailed for England in mid-November, Macdonald would have known how close his career had come to disaster. Had he been excluded from the final Confederation talks in London in 1866–67, he would hardly have become the Dominion's first prime minister.

Preparation of the new British American constitution fell into two parts, a debate on the blueprint among the colonial delegates themselves before Christmas, and negotiations with the British in the New Year to shape an act of Parliament. Thirteen delegates representing Canada, New Brunswick, and Nova Scotia began talks at London's Westminster Palace Hotel on December 4, 1866, concluding their deliberations on Christmas Eve. The politician who had so nearly been banned from taking part became, in the tribute of fellow delegate Hector Langevin, the key figure, "*l'homme* de la conférence." Indeed, his primacy was recognized at the outset, when the Maritimers proposed him as chairman. Maritime delegates also quietly accepted the Quebec scheme as the basis for discussion — there was no alternative blueprint. Delegates began with an outline survey of the seventy-two resolutions, deleting those that applied only to Newfoundland and Prince Edward Island, which had dropped out of the movement, and highlighting others for reconsideration. Then they started over again, working through the scheme in detail. In all, they sat for around sixty hours, allowing about fifty minutes to examine each resolution. The Maritimers were "excessively fond of talking" but few changes were made. Much of the credit went to the chairman, "un fin renard," Langevin called him, the elegant fox — well-informed, persuasive, capable, and popular. Macdonald's contribution was remarkable since, for much of the conference, he was in pain, having badly burned himself in a hotel-room fire.

After Christmas there was a lull, while the Colonial Office considered the delegates' work. Even Macdonald managed to take a short break in Paris. Then, as the February 1867 meeting of the Westminster Parliament approached, the pace quickened and the pressure intensified, with some disagreements between the delegates and British policy-makers. There were problems in turning the fuzzy edges of the "London Resolutions" into the sharp language of an act of Parliament, while British concerns, for instance about the role of the Senate, opened regional divisions and strained the harmony of December.

By January 13, 1867, Macdonald feared "a good deal of difficulty" with his francophone colleagues, Cartier and Langevin, over "the proposed change as to Property and Civil rights." It seems that the British were probing an overlap in the delegates' London Resolutions, which allocated responsibility for "Marriage and Divorce" to the central Parliament, but gave the provinces control over "Property and civil rights (including the solemnization of marriages)." As devout Catholics, French Canadians rejected divorce but they recognized that British North America's Protestant majority permitted the dissolution of failed marriages. Hence, in a very Canadian compromise, the central Parliament could grant divorces, but Lower Canada's legislature would have power to prevent Catholic divorcees from remarrying within the province.

If there was a row over marriage laws, it was soon settled, but it triggered a nasty conspiracy theory. When Cartier died in 1873, a Quebec journalist, Elzéar Gérin, claimed that the anglophone delegates in London tried to bully their two French colleagues into accepting a centralized union. But, said Gérin, Cartier outwitted them, by mobilizing the figurehead premier, Narcisse Belleau, who had been left behind in Canada. Belleau was warned to stand by for a telegram telling him to submit the Great Coalition's resignation, a nuclear option that would halt Confederation. Gérin had been sent to London to cover the talks, after serving a prison sentence in Ottawa for punching a politician. Since the delegates had agreed on complete secrecy, he relied on oblique briefings from Langevin. Gérin was not a reliable witness, and he likely exaggerated rumours of a brief row over marriage policy. The story surfaced again in 1886, after the hanging of Louis Riel. This time there was just one villain, who had allegedly conducted an insidious campaign to re-write the scheme. The slander still echoes: John A. Macdonald, the devious enemy of French Canada, allegedly plotted to twist Canada's constitution into a centralizing document that would destroy Quebec. The evidence proves this to be nonsense. Five drafts of the proposed constitution written between Christmas 1866 and February 9, 1867 survive. All are based on the London Resolutions, and there is no trace of the extensive restructuring required to impose centralized control.

These documents formed the basis for tense negotiations between the delegates and the British. Whitehall deputy minister Frederic Rogers, who had wanted Macdonald to dry out in Canada, now hailed him as "the ruling genius and spokesman" among the visitors. "I was very greatly struck by his power of management and adroitness." The French Canadians and the Maritimers were on guard against any damaging concession, "as eager dogs watch a rat hole," Rogers thought. Macdonald argued controversial points "with cool, ready fluency," determined to avoid "the slightest divergence from the narrow line already agreed" by his colleagues; "every word was measured ... while he was making for a point ahead, he was never for a moment unconscious of any of the rocks among which he had to steer." The British had found their strong man to lead the new Canada, but they did not tear up the agreed Confederation blueprint, nor did he ask them to do so.

Indeed, the British vetoed one of Macdonald's most fervent wishes, that the Confederation should be styled the "Kingdom of Canada." Fearful of upsetting the Americans, they preferred the term "Dominion." "A great opportunity was lost," Macdonald complained two decades later, but perhaps he won one minor victory in the naming stakes. British officials had assumed that Lower Canada would resume its historic name, Quebec, inferring from this that Upper Canada would become the province of Toronto. Macdonald's Kingston voters resented the upstart rival city, and he probably chose the unexpected name of "Ontario" for the revived province.

The finalized bill was introduced into Westminster on February 19 and passed into law, as the British North America Act, on March 29. The new Dominion would be launched on July 1, 1867. To Macdonald's admirers, he was "the artificer in chief," the vital craftsman without whom Confederation could not have happened. Others resented his primacy. Cartier had run huge risks managing "the fears, prejudices and jealousies of a proud and sensitive population" to bring French Canada into Confederation. Alexander Mackenzie, Canada's second prime minister, gave the credit for securing Upper Canadian support to his idol, George Brown. Just as John A. Macdonald had hijacked the clergy reserves issue, so he stole Confederation too. "Having no great work of his own to boast about, he bravely plucks the laurel from the brows of the actual combatants and real victors, and fastens it on his own head." This was unfair: Macdonald believed in Confederation, even if he was not starry-eyed about the challenge of joining Canada to Nova Scotia and New Brunswick, with their small populations and sluggish economies. When a supporter rejoiced that Confederation would free Upper Canadians from the "financial millstone" of French Canada, Macdonald sharply retorted: "Do you think you will be better off with three mill-stones around your neck instead of one?"

As leader of the British North American delegations creating a new nation, John A. Macdonald was working "from morning till night" in London through the winter of 1866–67. Yet, intriguingly, he also managed to get married. People fall in love at the most unexpected moments in life, so maybe there is no mystery about a widower of fifty-two finding himself suddenly swept away by a young woman twenty-two years his junior. Somehow he found time, during one of the busiest periods of his life, to woo Miss Agnes Bernard, and hurry her to the altar.

According to a well-informed early biographer, Macdonald proposed shortly before Christmas, but he mentioned no engagement when he wrote to his sister Louisa on December 27. Agnes probably accepted him early in January, and she became Mrs. John A. Macdonald on February 16, 1867.

Reared among Jamaica's privileged white minority, Agnes Bernard had come to Canada at seventeen. In 1858, her brother Hewitt became Macdonald's private secretary, and Agnes accompanied him, first to Toronto and then to Quebec City. Nicknamed "Pug," she was "clever, accomplished, and handsome" — but nobody called this rigidly serious young woman pretty. Agnes was a political groupie, sometimes following Assembly debates from the gallery: when she married, Gowan concluded that "the voice of the Chamber has indeed beguiled her." Macdonald had met her, but he kept a certain social distance from his secretary. In 1865, Agnes and her mother moved to England. Macdonald encountered them taking a stroll in London's West End one evening late in 1866. Since Hewitt Bernard was the conference secretary, their paths would probably have crossed anyway.

During his nine years as a widower, there had been rumours that John A. Macdonald would marry again, but he preferred the solitary life that had characterized much of his first marriage anyway. He felt crowded when a male relative visited him in Quebec in 1861. "I am now so much accustomed to live alone, that it frets me to have a person always in the same house with me." He may not have been entirely celibate. "We speak not of Mr. Macdonald's private life," the *Globe* had thundered with menacing hint as it denounced his drunkenness in 1866. The next year, an eccentric opponent listed adultery among his many sins. Yet, suddenly, he was married.

Courtesy of Topley Studio Fonds/Library and Archives Canada/PA-025366.

John A. Macdonald's second wife, Agnes Bernard, married him in 1867. "She had a good deal to put up with."

Late on December 11, 1866, a grey winter day, the delegates had returned to London after visiting Lord Carnarvon's country mansion ("one of the swellest places in England," Macdonald called it). To keep warm in his hotel room, Macdonald donned two nightshirts and then, as was his habit, he propped himself up in bed to read a newspaper. Tired from travel, he nodded off, dropping the paper on to a bedside candle. He was "awakened by intense heat" to find his bed on fire. "I didn't lose my presence of mind," he boasted. After emptying his water jug on to the flames, he ripped open the singed pillows, "poured an avalanche of feathers on the blazing mass, & then stamped out the fire with my hands & feet." Fearful that his mattress might still be smouldering, he roused Cartier and Galt from their adjoining bedrooms, and they brought their water jugs to soak his bed. Only then did he realize he was badly burned. Macdonald "very nearly lost his life," wrote Galt, and the victim agreed, "my escape was miraculous."

Significantly, the three decided to keep quiet about the episode. However, despite Macdonald's attempt to shrug off his injuries, he was confined to the hotel on doctor's orders, celebrating Christmas Day with tea and toast when its catering facilities shut down. There was no suggestion that he had been drunk, but when a man with a notorious alcohol problem catches fire in bed, speculation is obvious. If John A. Macdonald aimed to become Canada's first prime minister, he needed a twenty-four hour guard — and that meant finding a wife, fast.

Hewitt Bernard was appalled to learn that his boss aimed to become his brother-in-law. To his credit, he put his loyalty to Agnes first, claiming later that "he did everything he could to dissuade his sister from the marriage." Macdonald assured Bernard that "there could only be one objection; and he had promised reformation in that respect." Here was a dangerous ambiguity:

was Macdonald taking a wife to fight his alcohol problem, or giving up drink to get married? Agnes was thirty, the age when cruel chauvinism branded a single woman a failure in the marriage stakes. A strong believer in duty, she knew that she was taking on not just a husband but a job. In a stilted and sporadic diary that she later kept in Ottawa, she called herself "a great Premier's wife."

The wedding took place at very short notice. Macdonald claimed that the ceremony was hurried on so that Agnes could be presented to Queen Victoria, but it is equally likely that he needed to demonstrate possession of a wife to become Canada's first prime minister. The fashionable church of St George's, Hanover Square, was packed with friends of Canada: three of the four bridesmaids were delegates' daughters, giving the marriage the flavour of a dynastic alliance. As the couple took their vows, "a bright ray of sunshine fell through the fine old stained glass windows," lighting the scene in a happy omen. At the wedding breakfast, the bridegroom delivered a "brilliant speech," playing on the joke that he was applying the political principle of uniting the provinces to his domestic life — "Confederation, under a female sovereign." The couple's health was toasted by elder statesman Francis Hincks. Twelve years earlier, Macdonald had denounced him as "steeped to the lips in corruption." Now Hincks presented Agnes with a valuable diamond and pearl bracelet. The couple headed for a two-day honeymoon in Oxford: Macdonald was needed in London when the Confederation legislation came before Parliament.

The newlyweds were "kept in England by some Canadian business," which included a special audience with Queen Victoria, who praised the loyalty of her transatlantic subjects and the "very important measure" of Confederation. The prime minister-designate formally replied that Canadians had declared "in the most solemn & emphatic manner our resolve to be under the sovereignty of Your Majesty and your family forever." It was early May before the couple returned to Ottawa. On his first Monday back at work, Macdonald held a celebration luncheon. An Ottawa diarist was "very much disturbed" to learn that "John A. was carried out of the lunch room ... *hopelessly drunk.*" "What a prospect Mrs. John A. has before her!"

5

1867–1872
Gristle into Bone

"Except Macdonald, I know none of the Delegates who really think enough of the future," wrote Alexander Galt from London, adding that even Macdonald believed that the "immediate task is to complete the Union, leaving the rest to be solved by time." Lord Monck had commissioned Macdonald to form the first ministry, enabling him, as his friend Gowan urged, "to give a fair start to the new Dominion." Macdonald had claimed in 1866 that "a great party is arising of moderate men," soaring above "the petty politics of past days ... to join together for the good of the future of Canada." Unfortunately, the formation of the first Dominion Cabinet disproved this noble vision.

Macdonald nearly failed to shoehorn claimants and interest groups into the thirteen available Cabinet places. The Maritime premiers, Tupper and Tilley, each selected a colleague to fill the region's four seats. Tough bargaining allocated five ministers to Ontario against Quebec's four. Since the Conservatives were weak in Ontario, Macdonald reappointed all three Great Coalition Reformers. He also retained the courteous and bilingual Alexander Campbell to run the Senate. Campbell represented the Tory wing of the party: the prime minister was the only Macdonald Conservative in the Cabinet. His biggest headache lay in the political arithmetic of Quebec. Naturally, French Canadians claimed three of the four seats — leaving one ministry for the anglophone minority. D'Arcy McGee demanded the place on behalf of the Dominion's Irish Catholics, but his appointment would have excluded Quebec's Protestant community, whose spokesman, Galt, also represented Montreal finance. Macdonald confronted the impasse "in a constant state of partial intoxication," said Galt, and threatened to abandon his commission. The logjam was broken by Tupper, who persuaded McGee they should both stand down, freeing the thirteenth place for a Nova Scotian Irish Catholic. The Halifax merchant, Edward "Papa" Kenny, was surprised to receive the summons to Ottawa. To prevent the Grits from controlling the new province of Ontario, John A. Macdonald tried a new twist on an old triangular rivalry. To block George Brown, Sandfield Macdonald agreed to become his running mate as first premier of Ontario.

George-Étienne Cartier disliked playing second fiddle to the new prime minister, and resented Ontario's extra Cabinet place. On the first Dominion Day, July 1, 1867, the moment Gowan hoped Canada would escape from "a sea of strife and littleness," Cartier's resentment exploded. There were rumours that the British would mark Confederation by bestowing titles and medals, perhaps using the prestigious Order of the Bath, a relic of medieval locker-room culture when kings shared their ablutions with trusted retainers. A knight commander of the Bath outranked any ordinary "sir." "Come back a K.C.B.," Campbell had cheerfully urged the newlyweds, "Sir John and Lady Macdonald." The Bath included a category of "Companions," associate members who put the coveted letters "C.B." after their names. On the morning of July 1, Macdonald learned he was to be knighted: he promptly scribbled a note to Agnes, addressing the envelope to "Lady Macdonald." But when Cartier found he was only to receive a C.B, he angrily rejected the honour as a personal affront and an insult to Quebec. Galt reluctantly declined his C.B. too. In the coming months, knighthoods soothed the egos of Sir George and Sir Alexander, but the Dominion had made a sour start.

The limits on Macdonald's prime ministerial authority were underlined by his inability to save the Commercial Bank from collapse in October 1867 — a crash that almost bankrupted him. Kingston's bank had been over-extended for years, but its directors failed to crack down on unreliable borrowers — such as board member Sir John A. Macdonald, with his $80,000 overdraft. In October 1867, a run on deposits highlighted its vulnerability. Finance Minister Galt travelled to Montreal to beg Canada's bank bosses for help, but their bail-out terms were tough. Macdonald's Cabinet colleagues insisted that the package was "insufficient to warrant any action by Government," and the Commercial Bank closed its doors. Not only powerless to save his riding's bank, Macdonald also lost his finance minister. Galt resigned, expressing "exasperation" with Macdonald: "had he stood by the Bank as I did, it would have been saved." The wreckage was absorbed by a Montreal rival and Macdonald's debts fell into unfriendly hands.

The first Dominion Parliament assembled on November 7, 1867, with the new prime minister orchestrating the ceremonies. A journalist described him as "a young looking oldish man, dark hair, not quite as plentiful as it was ten years ago, a prominent nose, dark eyes, and a pliable and sagacious mouth." With Brown

absent, Cartier sulking, Galt marginalized and Sandfield neutral-
ized, Macdonald appeared dominant, but his position was weaker
than it seemed. Confederation itself remained insecure. Eighteen
of Nova Scotia's nineteen MPs demanded repeal of the union.
Macdonald believed that their leader, Joseph Howe, would "by
and by be open to reason" but, if statesmanship required patience,
politics might demand action. The session took its toll in a sadly
familiar manner. On December 16, a backbench MP spotted "Sir
John drinking" and rushed by cab to fetch Agnes.

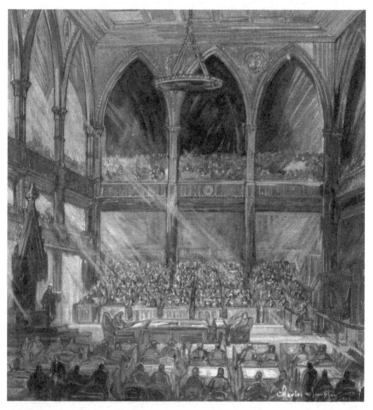

*The Dominion of Canada's first parliament looks like a dream come true
as it meets in November 1867.*

Agnes was learning about married life in a cramped house, shared with her mother and her brother, Macdonald's secretary, Hewitt Bernard. Sometimes she misread her husband's mood: once, he lost his temper when she teased him, and actually ordered her out of the room — although "the good old boy" quickly called her back. She tried to be an attentive spouse: Macdonald, she recognized, was "so busy and so much older than I that I would soon fall out of his life if I went my own ways." Agnes had enough self-knowledge to realize that her pride in being "the instrument of so much improvement" was partly "a love of power." She tried to ban politics on Sundays and chivvied her exhausted husband to attend church, but she abandoned her campaign for daily morning prayers: "Sir John rises late — it is his only quiet time ... he ought not to forego it."

Macdonald was still more likely to turn for support to the bottle than to his bride. In January 1868, Agnes enigmatically noted "a rather trying week," leading her to give up wine "for example's sake." The root problem, as their doctor warned, was that Macdonald was "working himself to death." Ottawa's primitive infrastructure also threatened his health: the Macdonalds' cesspit froze, causing an "insufferable" smell from blocked sewage. Late in February 1868, Canada's first prime minister told Alexander Campbell he was close to quitting. Campbell tried to cheer him: because Macdonald was "a little depressed," he was considering an option "which in moments of more robust health you would not contemplate." Campbell hoped Macdonald would not retire, "but if on mature consideration ... you should really set about such a move," the obvious answer was to appoint himself lieutenant-governor of Ontario. The job would provide "ease and quiet" and, equally important, it would remove Macdonald from Ottawa. "You have filled too large a space in our horizon to adopt the plan of occupying an independent seat in Parliament — of necessity, you must either lead for the government or opposition." It was the first attempt to find a way out for the politician who dominated public life. A career as a lawyer was no longer attractive, and he did not wish to become a judge. When well-wishers suggested he should appoint himself to the judicial bench, he replied that he would rather go to Hell. The exit strategy problem was never solved, and Sir John A. Macdonald carried on until he died.

When Parliament was sitting, Agnes waited up to welcome her husband back from late-night sittings. Macdonald was in "cheery" form when he came home around 2:00 a.m. on April 7, 1868, full of a ringing speech by D'Arcy McGee pleading for harmony with the discontented Nova Scotians. Suddenly "a low, rapid knocking at the front door" brought terrible news: McGee had been shot dead by terrorists. Hours of horror and days of fear ensued. "John's face was white with fatigue, sleeplessness and regret," Agnes wrote, but "he never gave in or complained." The tragedy brought them close together: within a few weeks, Agnes was pregnant.

Political insecurities abounded. In February and March 1868, the still-resentful Cartier explored the possibility of an alliance with George Brown. The feelers lapsed because Brown was busy expanding the *Globe*, but it triggered unsettling rumours. There was friction too with Sandfield Macdonald in Ontario. Foreseeing tensions between centre and periphery, Sir John A. made it clear that he would strike down objectionable provincial laws. "By a firm yet patient course, I think the Dominion must win in the long run." Sandfield complained that he was not consulted on important matters, yet it was his namesake who was blamed when the Ontario government controversially decided to axe grants to denominational colleges. Sir John privately denounced Sandfield as "bigoted and exceedingly narrow-minded" on the issue, but he confessed himself "quite powerless in the matter," even though the funding cut impacted upon Queen's, in his Kingston riding. The Ontario government, he admitted, was "very jealous of anything like dictation on our part." Meanwhile, the *Globe* denounced Sandfield as Ottawa's puppet.

Nova Scotia remained the main challenge. Macdonald sought to avoid confrontation but aimed to seize the right moment to seek compromise, branding Tupper's plans to barnstorm the province with pro-Confederation oratory as "zeal without discretion." Nova Scotian political culture worked in his favour: Bluenoses were vocally loyal to Britain, preferring, as Joseph Howe put it, London under John Bull to Ottawa under Jack Frost. But when John Bull refused to release them from Confederation, they faced a choice between revolution and compromise. Nova Scotia had rejected revolution in 1776, and Howe was too old to fight now. Everything depended on timing, and John A. Macdonald was an expert at combining long periods of patience with sudden bursts of decisive activity.

The moment of greatest danger also presented the best opportunity to seek agreement. In August 1868, anti-Confederation members of the Dominion and provincial legislatures gathered in Halifax in an ominously titled "convention," which might even declare Nova Scotian independence. Hastily, Sir John A. Macdonald assembled a high-powered delegation, with Sandfield as his prize exhibit — the former opponent of Confederation who was now running the Dominion's largest province. Agnes came along too. Although her pregnancy was only confirmed after her return ("the Blessing from on high, has been with us," as she put it), she had felt queasy back in June, but blamed the sultry Ottawa climate. Her presence signalled that Macdonald had come in friendship. The "convention" failed to trap the visitors into formal negotiations, as if they represented a foreign power, but Macdonald jollied its members, offering to remedy practical grievances. The mission enabled Howe to strike a face-saving deal — and even enter Macdonald's Cabinet. In June 1869, the Dominion Parliament approved "better terms" for Nova Scotia. Extra money was thrown at the province — and the Grits reminded Ontario taxpayers that they provided the cash.

"I have never seen my husband in such cheery moods," Agnes noted as she welcomed new Cabinet recruit Joseph Howe to dinner in January 1869. Within weeks, their world came crashing down. Agnes gave birth to a girl on February 8, after an excruciating labour: little Mary had an enlarged head, which was soon diagnosed as hydrocephalus, "water on the brain." The Macdonalds faced the tragedy that their daughter would suffer mobility problems and probably impaired mental development too. For Agnes, Mary's disability was a divine message, although its meaning was not clear. "Only teach me, Heavenly Father, to see the lesson it was destined to teach." The occasional joyful outbursts that punctuated her first two years of marriage were replaced by the stern, grey discipline of two lives yoked together by a handicapped daughter. There were no more children.

While Macdonald digested the terrible news that his daughter would never live a normal life, a second blow fell. His massive overdraft was now controlled by Montreal banker, Hugh Allan. In April 1869, Allan called in the debt. It totalled just short of $80,000, ten times Macdonald's annual salary as prime minister. This was a heavy blow but not a complete disaster: his law firm still reaped income from its Trust and Loan Company business. Hewitt Bernard had insisted on a marriage settlement for

Agnes, a kind of Victorian "pre-nup," to protect her own capital from Macdonald's creditors. But paying off the overdraft wiped out Macdonald's property portfolio. Aged fifty-four, and given contemporary life expectancy, Sir John A. Macdonald could not count on many active years to rebuild his savings and provide for his handicapped child. Retirement now seemed impossible.

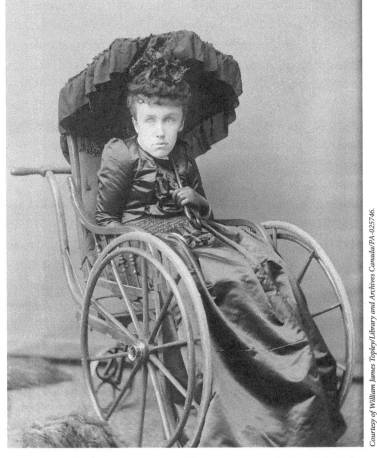

Macdonald's daughter, Mary, 1893. Still in mourning for her father, this photograph fails to capture her happy personality.

Courtesy of William James Topley/Library and Archives Canada/PA-025746.

Macdonald responded to the double disaster with a series of embarrassing binges. The *Globe* later alleged that he drank heavily during the summer of 1869, although there was then "no unusual pressure upon Ministers." In October, Macdonald "committed himself disgracefully" at an official luncheon in Toronto in honour of Queen Victoria's second son, Prince Arthur: his minder, Hewitt Bernard, was "kept in a state of miserable anxiety about Sir John" throughout the trip. Agnes initially blamed her own "over-anxiety" for her husband's lapses, but on November 7, 1869, she faced the failure of the matrimonial pact of 1867. "I was overconfident, vain, presumptuous in my sense of power. I fancied I could do much, and I failed signally."

Macdonald's binge-drinking erupted just as Canada was about to take a mighty leap to the Rocky Mountains. After negotiations in London, the Dominion purchased the territorial rights of the Hudson's Bay Company (covering the future provinces of Manitoba, Saskatchewan, and Alberta), with the transfer date set for December 1, 1869. Aboriginal people were ignored in the deal. So too was the small Red River settler community. Half of its 11,000 population were French-speaking Catholic Métis, descendants of European fur-traders and Native women, known by the racist term "half-breeds." The remainder were English-speaking Métis, plus about 1,500 recent arrivals, mostly from Ontario. Generally contemptuous of the Métis, the incomers were disruptive but too few to seize control.

Ottawa's first governor was William McDougall, a Reformer and Macdonald's Cabinet colleague since 1864. He travelled through the United States, with orders to keep a low profile until he received confirmation of the December 1 transfer. On November 2, his route to the Red River was blocked by French Métis, and he retreated to the Minnesota border town of Pembina. McDougall's communications with Ottawa were slow but, thanks to the transatlantic cable, the Canadian government could urgently contact Britain. When Macdonald learned of McDougall's setback, he cabled London to delay the transfer: Canada would only accept the territory when Britain had pacified its inhabitants. However, McDougall knew nothing of this and, on December 1, acting on his own initiative, he proclaimed himself governor of the Northwest. Believing that he was filling a vacuum, MacDougall in fact created one, by prematurely proclaiming the end of the Company control without being able to assert his own authority. As Macdonald realized, under international law, the Red River people were now entitled to establish their own government — which the Americans might recognize. McDougall probably expected that the "Canadian party" would rally to his proclamation and install him as governor. In fact it was the francophone Métis who took control.

In 1868, Macdonald had pacified 370,000 Nova Scotians. In 1869 he stumbled into a dangerous confrontation with a few thousand people at the distant Red River. Contrasting cultures explained the difference. Nova Scotians made speeches and passed resolutions; Métis armed themselves to hunt buffalo. Macdonald met with frowns in Halifax; McDougall was confronted with firearms. Macdonald had ruthlessly sidelined Nova Scotia's Unionist minority; in the Red River, the "Canadian party" were both arrogant and inept. The dominant figure in Nova Scotia, Joseph Howe, was a veteran and skilled politician; his counterpart in the Red River was the twenty-four-year-old Louis Riel, catapulted into leadership because he had studied, unsuccessfully, for the Catholic priesthood in Montreal. Above all, Macdonald controlled policy towards Nova Scotia himself, travelling to Halifax when he judged the moment right to strike a deal. But the Red River was inaccessible, especially during the winter, and he had to work through William McDougall.

Macdonald grumbled that the stand-off was "a most inglorious *fiasco*," and he censured McDougall for exceeding instructions. But, as prime minister, Sir John A. Macdonald was responsible for appointing someone notorious for out-spoken inflexibility. In 1861, McDougall had controversially threatened to "look to Washington" to secure representation by population. He had called French Canadians "a foreign race" with an alien religion. Métis distrust was further aroused by his actions, as a member of Sandfield Macdonald's ministry in 1862, in strong-arming the Ojibwa into allowing settlement on Manitoulin, the giant island in Lake Huron. McDougall was an obsessive expansionist, driven by a sense of mission: in the year before his appointment, he had survived a serious illness and the unexpected death of his wife. Although Macdonald assured McDougall that he had "every confidence in your pru-dence and tact" in managing the transition to Canadian rule, the truth was he had made a totally unsuitable appointment. Equally unfortunate was Macdonald's failure to foresee the communications problem: arrangements should have been made to send coded telegrams to St Paul, Minnesota, and rush them by courier on to Pembina.

Macdonald also blamed the "supineness" of the Hudson's Bay Company officials. "They gave us no notice of any feeling of discontent at the change." But everybody knew that Company rule had been somnolent for decades, and Macdonald had made little effort to find out about the Northwest. "We are in a blissful state of ignorance as to what the requirements of that country may be," he remarked to a job-seeker early in November 1869 — remarkably casual preparation for the annexation of two million square kilometres. Indeed, Canada's advance moves had been counterproductive: Métis suspicions were aroused by survey teams, sent to forestall claim-jumping squatters. Most bizarre was the appearance of Joseph Howe at the Red River in October 1869 on a personal fact-finding visit, his very presence a reminder that Nova Scotian discontent had forced concessions from the Dominion. Howe should either have been sent with an Ottawa welcome pack, or discouraged from travelling altogether. When trouble broke out, Macdonald called the Métis "these poor people ... handed over like a flock of sheep," but his own failure to engage with the Red River community had precipitated the crisis.

Through the winter of 1869–70, there were almost too many negotiators shuttling in slow motion over two thousand kilometres between Ottawa and the Red River, sometimes on overlapping missions. Suddenly, Riel upped his demands, insisting that the eleven thousand people should become a full province — and so the Red River became Manitoba. The convoluted negotiations left one dangerous issue unresolved. Ottawa wisely signalled that a blind eye would be turned to the extra-legal activities of Riel's provisional government. But how far could that amnesty extend? The issue was highlighted by the tragic death of Thomas Scott. A young Irish Protestant who had arrived via Ontario, Scott was imprisoned for opposing Riel. Openly contemptuous of his French-speaking Catholic captors, Scott was court-martialled for insubordination — and sentenced to death. Unwisely believing that it would strengthen his authority, Riel confirmed the execution. On March 4, 1870, Scott was shot by firing squad, although there were rumours that he was still alive when dumped in his coffin, and that his body was contemptuously thrown into an icy river. Ontario honoured him as a slaughtered Orangeman. The Catholic bishop, Alexandre-Antonin Taché, reached Red River four days after Scott's killing, bearing Macdonald's verbal assurance (not quite a binding promise) of a general amnesty — but Ontario would not forget what it regarded as cold-blooded murder.

By late April, 1870, Parliament in Ottawa was waiting for the prime minister to introduce legislation to create the new province. But, suddenly, Macdonald's Commons attendance became "very irregular": reports that he was "indisposed" caused "much comment and speculation." Tired and in poor health, he had gone on a bender. News even filtered back to England where one politician noted that, generally, "no especial notice" was taken in Ottawa of Macdonald's twice-yearly binges. The complaint on this occasion was not that he was drunk for a whole week but rather "that he should not have waited till the urgent business ... was disposed of."

The *Globe* was less philosophical. In a leader headed "A Foul Disgrace," it charged that Macdonald had "again yielded to the temptation of drink." No other country would tolerate its prime minister "staggering" around the parliamentary bar, "babbling in maudlin intoxication" as his colleagues steered him to safety. Since "Sir John A. Macdonald's drinking fits usually last for some little time," nobody knew how long he would "leave the affairs of the country to look after themselves." Two days later, the inebriate managed to introduce the Manitoba Bill but the *Globe* kept up a sustained denunciation that few politicians could survive.

Suddenly, it was not Macdonald's career that was threatened, but his life. He had returned to his desk after a Cabinet meeting on Friday afternoon, May 6, 1870. From his adjoining office, Hewitt Bernard heard a strange noise and found Canada's prime minister writhing in agony on the floor. Macdonald's underlying health problem was finally diagnosed: he had been felled by a gallstone, much of it still trapped in his system. With a barely detectable pulse, John A. Macdonald seemed to be dying. Parliament adjourned; an Ottawa newspaper typeset an eight-column obituary. Agnes converted Macdonald's office into a sickroom where he remained for almost three weeks, with bursts of pain so severe that morphine injections were required. Recovery was slow. Early in June, he was carried the short distance to the apartment of the Speaker of the Commons, and on fine days he was wheeled to the cliff overlooking the Ottawa River. The first, dangerous experiments in gallbladder surgery lay a decade in the future, so his diet had to be tightly controlled. Limiting him to half an oyster as a treat, his doctor sternly reminded him that "the hopes of Canada" depended upon Macdonald's survival: Sir John A. was amused at the hopes of Canada depending upon half an oyster.

Macdonald's illness reminded Canadians that they appreciated him and needed him. Luther Holton, who had often clashed with him, expressed "the highest admiration" and "the warmest personal regard" for the stricken prime minister. As the *Montreal Gazette* sympathetically observed, "few have any notion of the wear and tear of mind, and downright fag work" of Cabinet ministers "from early morn till late at night. It is a constant strain." Macdonald seemed "to divine by the intuition of genius what he could and what he could not do" in managing Parliament, returning good humoured replies to the most insulting provocations.

In July, Macdonald escaped the heat of Ottawa for a summer of convalescence on Prince Edward Island, which was still not part of the Dominion. Perhaps the journey stimulated memories of travelling with Isabella in her illness, while the route retraced that optimistic mission just six years earlier to woo the Maritimers into Confederation at Charlottetown. He spent two months incommunicado in the Gulf, but likely had informal discussions with pro-Confederation politician John Hamilton Gray, who welcomed him to the island. In late September, feeling "*nearly* as strong as before my illness," Macdonald returned to a "gratifying" welcome in Montreal. His resolve to take things easy "for some months" did not last long: the following April, he admitted that "after my long illness, I was overwhelmed with arrears of work."

As Macdonald faced death, admirers became aware of his losses in the Commercial Bank crash. Toronto businessman David Macpherson organized a testimonial fund, to ensure that Agnes would not be left a penniless widow. Macdonald was not unique in being the beneficiary of such generosity: D'Arcy McGee and Liberal leader Alexander Mackenzie also received public subscriptions, and even the ultra-virtuous George Brown accepted supporters' cash to develop the *Globe*. Formally launched in November 1870, the campaign raised two-thirds of its $100,000 target. To safeguard his wife and child — not least from Macdonald's own financial recklessness — the fund was controlled by trustees. "All the men whom John A. has helped into office are expected to subscribe," sneered the *Globe*. In fact, the indirect relationship spared Macdonald from conflict-of-interest issues. Far from encouraging "a lively sense of favours to come," he took a tough line with Macpherson over the Pacific Railway soon afterwards. Indeed, the big loser from Macdonald's health crisis was the *Globe* itself, furious — as a rival newspaper put it — that its target had been "snatched from the very mouth of the grave." Twice in four years, it had broken the taboos and denounced his weakness for the bottle. Twice Macdonald had escaped. He still had to tackle his alcohol problem, but it was now less likely that journalists would risk raising the issue.

Despite the wave of goodwill, Macdonald's political problems remained challenging. While he was ill, a delegation from British Columbia had arrived, via California, to agree terms for admission to Confederation as Canada's sixth province. During the negotiations, carried on just yards from Macdonald's sickroom, Cartier offered to build a transcontinental railway. Macdonald would have approved. The Red River crisis had persuaded him that the Americans would "do all they can" to grab the Northwest, and Canadians must "show unmistakeably our resolve to build the Pacific Railway." But the expansive Cartier added a condition that the cautious Macdonald later downplayed: the railway would be started within two years and finished within ten. This timetable was unrealistic: no route had been surveyed, and nobody knew how to build through the mountains. For British Columbians, of course, Cartier's promise was engraved in stone, and would cause problems in the years ahead.

Macdonald's weakness in his home province was greater than ever, and his coalition strategy was coming apart. Of the three Ontario Reformers appointed to Cabinet in 1867, Fergusson-Blair had died (aged only fifty-two), Howland had become Ontario's lieutenant-governor and McDougall had gone to the Red River and off the political rails. Opponents gibed that the stray Reformers Macdonald gobbled up since 1854 rarely lasted long, and now he found it hard to attract replacements. In 1869, he resorted to the ploy of recruiting Francis Hincks, who had been out of politics (indeed, mostly out of Canada) since ceasing to be premier fifteen years earlier. Macdonald explained away his 1854 slating of Hincksite corruption as a criticism of his Cabinet, not of Hincks himself. Appointed to the demanding portfolio of finance minister at the age of sixty-one, Hincks had little energy for political campaigning, and his resurrection struck few chords among Reformers.

The addition of the veteran Hincks cost Macdonald the support of thirty-three-year-old Richard Cartwright, nephew of John S. Cartwright, the Kingston Tory of his early years. Although a Macdonald supporter since his first election in 1863, the younger Cartwright could not swallow Hincks. Cartwright's defection highlighted another weakness. Macdonald and Campbell, the only two Ontario Conservatives in Cabinet, were both from Kingston, now a far smaller city than Toronto. In 1866, Macdonald had told an importunate supporter that "as soon as Toronto returns Conservative members, it will get Conservative appointments, but not before." Toronto had indeed elected hungry Conservatives to the first Dominion Parliament, and Cartwright had no chance of ever becoming the third Cabinet minister from Ontario's fifth largest city. In 1873, in a logical trajectory, Cartwright became Kingston's minister in a Liberal Cabinet.

The alliance of the two Macdonalds was also under strain. In 1869, a revolt in the Ontario legislature forced Sandfield to support a motion condemning Nova Scotia's "better terms," but he was still widely condemned as the puppet of his Ottawa namesake. In March 1870, Sandfield even talked of reuniting the Reform party, but the blunt truth was that he was now more valuable to the Grits as a fall guy than as a friend. Yet Sir John A. still needed him. As he put it, "Confederation is only yet in the gristle, and it will require five years more before it hardens into bone." To make that happen, both Macdonalds would have to win fresh terms of office in elections due by 1872.

The prime minister needed to spend 1871 strengthening his political base. Instead, he spent several months of that year in a triangular diplomatic struggle, defending Canada's interests in Washington against the United States and Britain. During the 1861–65 Civil War, Britain's aristocratic elite had openly sympathized with the South — even foolishly allowing the Confederates to build two warships in British shipyards. One of these, the *Alabama*, inflicted much damage on Northern commerce, and American politicians demanded reparations. Canada had its agenda too: compensation for the Fenian raids plus a trade pact to replace the Reciprocity Treaty that the United States had ended in 1866. That treaty had opened Canadian inshore waters to American fishermen, who continued to make incursions even after the agreement lapsed. Empire and Republic agreed to negotiate their differences, and London saw a simple solution: American grievances could be appeased by Canadian concessions. The British duly invited Canada's prime minister to accept the unprecedented honour of inclusion in the imperial diplomatic mission.

Macdonald saw the trap: he would be outvoted in the negotiating team. He was also wary about leaving Ottawa while Parliament was sitting. "My experience has been that when the Directing mind is removed, things always go wrong." But Canada's prime minister could not refuse to protect Canada's interests. Accompanied by Agnes, he spent almost three months in Washington. He complained that "the embarrassments & difficulties of my position were almost ... beyond endurance." The Americans refused to discuss the Fenians and offered no trade concessions. Relations with the British delegates were also tense, especially when Macdonald went over their heads to force London to agree that the Dominion Parliament must ratify

Canadian concessions: "treachery" grumbled the head of the mission; "struggling in muddy water with sharks" was Macdonald's description. Since the Dominion had no navy to enforce its rights, he had to accept a cash payment permitting Americans to access the fisheries. Disgusted with the terms, Macdonald considered refusing to sign the Treaty, but he realized this would have guaranteed its rejection in the U.S. Senate.

Even before he left Washington, Macdonald launched a two-pronged strategy to turn a dire situation around. In a remarkable piece of Dominion-wide news management, he persuaded pro-government papers not to comment on the agreement "until the *Globe* commits itself against the treaty.... if Brown finds I am opposed to the treaty, he may try to find reasons for supporting it." Simultaneously, he pressured the British, demanding a "liberal offer" to persuade Canada's Parliament to ratify. British politicians were outraged: this was ungentlemanly, it was blackmail — but, eventually, they agreed to guarantee a $2.5 million loan, money that Macdonald needed as a cash grant to launch the Pacific Railway. In an impressive marathon speech in May 1872, he persuaded Parliament to accept the Treaty "with all its imperfections ... for the sake of peace," as a patriotic sacrifice to "the great Empire of which we form a part." He could now turn to the transcontinental railway. Two syndicates were bidding for the project — one based in Montreal and headed by Hugh Allan, the other from Toronto led by David Macpherson. Worryingly, Allan was also backed by American investors but Macdonald hoped to persuade him to drop them and form an all-Canadian company by merging with Macpherson. As he remarked, "I have always been able to look a little ahead." Unfortunately, Allan and Macpherson squabbled and, facing into a general election, Macdonald lacked the time for delicate ego-management.

The Washington Treaty episode had undermined Macdonald in crucial respects. He had regarded it as "rather a dangerous experiment" to leave Ottawa while Parliament was sitting, and, subsequently, he felt that his hold over backbenchers had weakened. Absence also added to his admitted "neglect" of his own Kingston riding. But the biggest setback was the defeat of his allies in Ontario. Sir John A. Macdonald's departure for Washington coincided with the start of the provincial election campaign. Sandfield's ministry lost seats, some of which Macdonald believed would have been saved if he had campaigned himself. Sandfield was left leading a minority government but, in the eight months before the legislature met, he did little to strengthen his position. In December 1871, he was defeated, and the Reformers took over Ontario.

Characteristically, the prime minister pretended to regard the interlopers as a temporary nuisance whom he would soon dislodge. In fact, the Liberals (as they were increasingly called) would control Ontario until 1905. It was a sea change in Canadian politics, the replacement of Macdonald's ideal of an Ottawa-Ontario partnership by institutionalized confrontation between Dominion and its largest province. Ontario now banned politicians from sitting in both parliaments: Oliver Mowat emerged as provincial premier, Alexander Mackenzie as opposition leader in Ottawa. One of the biggest challenges facing Sir John A. Macdonald fighting the 1872 Dominion election was the hostility of Canada's strongest provincial government.

Macdonald started planning the campaign a year ahead. He claimed to be "in very good health" even though "the severe attack I had last year has left its mark on me for life." He was determined "to complete the work of Confederation before I make my final bow," and felt confident of winning a second term. Regarding Ontario as "the only difficulty," he mounted a counter-attack against the *Globe*. Once before, in 1858, Macdonald had attempted to establish a rival newspaper in Toronto, but he learned from the rapid collapse of the *Atlas* that any such venture needed careful planning — and capital. The launch of the Toronto *Mail* was a major enterprise, requiring the backing of wealthy supporters on the eve of an expensive election campaign. A bumptious young Englishman, T.C. Patteson, was appointed editor, but Macdonald micro-managed the project from Ottawa. "The first number was a good one," he congratulated Patteson, *"for a first number."* No doubt the *Mail* had to "assume an appearance of dignity at the outset," but it must "put *on* the war paint ... scalps *must* be taken." It would be some years before the *Mail* effectively challenged the *Globe*, but at least Macdonald now had a voice in the Ontario capital.

The 1872 election campaign was "hard and unpleasant." In two months, he delivered one hundred speeches across Ontario: "I have never worked so hard before." With voting spread out over several weeks, Macdonald planned (as in 1857) to start with his own triumphant return for Kingston, but the strategy came unstuck. Discovering that he was in trouble in the riding, Macdonald was forced to suspend his province-wide campaign to scramble for votes against John Carruthers, a respected local businessman. On the hustings, Macdonald charged his opponent with profiteering at the expense of Kingston consumers. When Carruthers indignantly denied the allegation, the prime minister of Canada slapped him in the face. Under pressure, Macdonald ("much excited," as the journalistic code put it) was drinking again. He won, but only by 735 votes to 604. He owed his victory to Catholic voters, who backed him by 250 votes to 78. The Protestant powerbase that had elected him since 1844 had narrowly turned against him.

After securing Kingston, Macdonald then resumed campaigning across the province, "more or less under the influence
of wine," Campbell alleged. Every riding had to be fought in
the "stern and up-hill battle" throughout Ontario. On the eve
of the campaign, disgusted at the demands of Prince Edward
County Conservative candidate J.S. McCuaig, he had written
off the riding. "I would prefer losing the seat to being bullied
by Master McCuaig." But he spoke for his greedy standard-
bearer, in a speech of two hours and twenty minutes at Picton,
and offered him a $1,000 campaign contribution: "You had
better spend it between nomination and polling." McCuaig
lost anyway. The Ontario government mobilized "its power,
patronage and influence," making the election campaign
frighteningly expensive. Timber barons subscribed lavishly
to Liberal funds to safeguard future logging concessions, and
Macdonald resorted to desperate measures to match opposition financial firepower. Alexander Campbell was shocked
to learn that his brother had done "a very foolish thing." A
Toronto businessman, Charles Campbell had been pressured
into guaranteeing a $10,000 bank loan, his only security
being Macdonald's promise of repayment "as a member of
the Government." Naively, Charley wondered "how far such
official promises are reliable." Macdonald also solicited contributions from wealthy businessmen. Humiliatingly, he begged
election funds from Hugh Allan, the banker who had called
in his overdraft. Accepting Allan's money also created a conflict of interest since the government was negotiating with him
over the Pacific Railway. Worse still, Cartier was in trouble in
Montreal East, where Allan was rumoured to have driven a
hard bargain — campaign cash in return for the contract on
his terms. In fact, Allan failed to save Cartier's seat, but his

estimated donations of $160,000 — equal to many millions today — were not likely to have been unconditional. In the last days of the campaign, Macdonald successfully begged "another ten thousand" from Allan. "Will be the last time of calling. Do not fail me," his telegram pleaded. He had no idea what Cartier had promised, and he would indeed be haunted by fears that he might have incautiously committed himself to some damaging pledge — just as he had trapped Charley Campbell into endorsing that $10,000 loan. Throughout the campaign, so Charles Tupper said, Macdonald was "upon the drink" and Campbell feared that he had "no clear recollection of what he did."

Macdonald saved forty of Ontario's eighty-eight seats, but he claimed to have won "as large or a larger majority" overall than in 1867. He regarded thirty-four out of the thirty-seven members from Nova Scotia and New Brunswick as sympathetic, whatever their party affiliation. However, Macdonald's calculation relied on the assumption that "independent members, or loose fish" would back him. When the new Parliament assembled in March 1873, ministers won Commons divisions by sixteen and twenty-five votes, well short of the fifty-six seat majority he had boasted. In reality, his position was barely secure. Just 104 out of 200 MPs labelled themselves as Conservatives. Effectively, Macdonald had given himself a ten-seat bonus, by allocating six constituencies to British Columbia and four to Manitoba, far more than their populations merited. All ten Western representatives sought favours from government, but they faced huge travel problems, and might not attend the entire parliamentary session. Opposition disunity helped him: twenty of the thirty-seven Maritime MPs were Liberals, but many distrusted the "Ontario First" aura around opposition leader Alexander Mackenzie. However, a dramatic issue might unite them in outrage, and a major scandal was about to break. In November 1873, eight months into the new Parliament, Sir John A. Macdonald was forced to resign, and his career seemed to be finished.

6

1872–1877
John A. Beats the Devil

Following his narrow victory in the 1872 election, Macdonald's priority was the Pacific Railway project. Neither Allan's election contributions nor Macpherson's testimonial fund influenced his judgment. Although Macpherson refused to merge with his rival, the contract went to Allan on Macdonald's terms: the Montreal entrepreneur dumped his American backers and formed the required all-Canadian company. In December, Macdonald assured *Mail* editor Patteson that "we have no rocks ahead for the next session." Unfortunately, Allan's American friends were outraged at their abandonment: they felt they had bought Allan, Allan had bought the election, and they wanted a slice of the contract. Macdonald rebuffed them, so they turned to the opposition. On April 2, 1873, a Liberal MP, L.S. Huntington, charged that the Pacific Railway project had been sold for election funds. Macdonald was able to reject the allegation by a thirty-one vote majority but, seven months later, Canada's first prime minister resigned in disgrace.

The "Pacific Scandal" (or "Slander" as Macdonald called it) was drawn out in instalments, each fresh wave of revelations fostering the impression of deeper corruption. The government prudently conceded a parliamentary committee but technical difficulties over its enquiry powers spurred paranoid accusations of a double-cross. On July 4, Huntington released Allan's correspondence with his American backers, carefully edited to increase its impact. Two weeks later, the *Globe* and the Montreal *Herald* published embarrassing documents stolen from the office of Allan's solicitor, J.J.C. Abbott (who would succeed Macdonald as prime minister in 1891). This scoop included the telegram from Macdonald to Allan begging for election funds: "I must have another ten thousand." In August, the prime minister established a three-person Royal Commission, with sweeping powers of investigation, but protecting himself by appointing J.R. Gowan, who was noted for his "friendship, almost amounting to affection, for Sir John A. Macdonald." The commission heard evidence throughout September, with Macdonald personally cross-examining witnesses. There was no formal proof of corruption, but plenty of sleazy detail about how elections were financed. For months, the government was constantly on the defensive.

The scandal was especially damaging because it could be reduced to a simple issue: even schoolchildren abused the Conservatives as "Charter-sellers." It also coincided with technical improvements in printing which effectively introduced political cartooning to Canada. The satirical magazine *Grip*, launched in May 1873, found Macdonald's huge nose and wild hair an easy target for caricature: a child in the street once pointed him out as "the bad man in *Grip*." The Royal Commission was portrayed as three smirking Macdonalds.

The prime minister was shown scattering pledges in a drunken spree, and haughtily stating, "I took the money and bribed the electors with it. Is there anything wrong with *that*?" That charge was unfair: he had begged election funds to pay campaign expenses not to bribe voters, although at ground level the difference was perhaps slight. However, even Macdonald acknowledged that his dealings with Allan *looked* bad. In England, the two parties raised election funds through arm's-length organizations, so that Disraeli and Gladstone, the Empire's great statesmen, never knew who financed their campaigns; in Canada, the party leader was his own bagman. As the October meeting of Parliament approached, the governor general, Lord Dufferin, warned Macdonald that his dealings with Allan "cannot but fatally affect your position as minister."

Macdonald alternated between denial and oblivion. In June, 1873, he suggested to his Cabinet colleagues that he should resign, "his idea being to keep them in office from the back benches" but, as Dufferin commented, "his Government would not last a day without him." His colleagues thought so too. "They almost told me that if I would not fight it out with them, they would not fight at all," he recalled. "I gave in." He retreated on vacation to Rivière-du-Loup. Alarmed by rumours of a breaking story, T.C. Patteson travelled from Toronto to ask Macdonald how the *Mail* should respond to opposition charges. "He laughed and said they knew nothing to tell." On his return journey, Patteson saw the "$10,000" telegram scoop in the *Globe*. "I felt very angry with Sir John A. for having deceived me."

In fact, Macdonald feared that the opposition knew too much. In May, "terribly over worked and harassed," he went on a binge. In June, the governor general reported a "very distressing and pitiable" discussion, in which the two men confirmed a death sentence on a woman who had killed her abusive husband — his hangover, her hanging. Early in August, Dufferin reported that "Sir John has been constantly drinking during the last month" and "in a terrible state for some time past." For a few days nobody — Agnes included — knew his whereabouts, and a story circulated that he had tried to drown himself in the St. Lawrence at Rivière-du-Loup. Macdonald would later cite the tale as evidence of his enemies' dishonesty, but perhaps it reflected some alcoholic episode of desperate self-harm. He was certainly behaving like somebody with a guilty conscience.

Two deaths in London, England — one of a colleague and the other of a project — added to his problems. Cartier had travelled to Britain to seek last-ditch medical treatment for his shattered health, and died there in May 1873. Macdonald was devastated, although his claim that they had "never had a serious difference" during their two-decade partnership was a pious exaggeration. As Dufferin noted, Allan was now "at liberty to make any statement he may please" about Cartier's alleged promises. But Allan, also in England, found himself presiding over the institutional funeral. His Pacific Railway needed British investment, but London financiers were distrustful of the scheme's murky aura. In October 1873, Allan admitted failure and surrendered his charter. Macdonald had nothing to show for the stench of the Pacific Scandal.

Even so, many believed the government could still survive when Parliament began debating Mackenzie's censure motion on October 27. "Macdonald's hold upon the affection of the people is very strong," Dufferin had noted. "Personally he is very popular, even among his opponents." Canadians believed that "the Dominion owes its existence" to Macdonald's "skill, talent and statesmanship." If he had spoken early in the debate, some said he would have won by at least ten votes. But having begun the session well, "after two or three days the strain became too much for him" and he took to drink, ignoring "the angry entreaties of his friends." In a formal debate, MPs could speak only once. Macdonald wanted to reply to the leading opposition orator, Edward Blake, "but — calculating on the effect of his physical infirmities breaking his adversary down — Blake determined to hold back." Privately, Macdonald feared the disclosure of some further incriminating document. Meanwhile, as an Ottawa diarist put it, "'ratting' goes on daily" as MPs fell away "like autumn leaves." Agnes broke gender restrictions to lobby one wavering government supporter, but he "ratted" too.

By the time Macdonald spoke, on November 3, his reticence seemed an admission of guilt. Pale and frail from exhaustion and booze, he nonetheless delivered a five-hour oration. A Cabinet colleague was persuaded to pass him glasses of neat gin, a transparent spirit that conveniently resembles water: it was said that Macdonald had two more suppliers, none of them knowing of the others' existence. For once, alcohol proved not a handicap but a fuel, for he closed with a dignified peroration. "I have fought the battle of Confederation," he claimed, as he looked beyond the parliamentary vote to the judgment of the people and the verdict of history. Nobody had "given more of his time, more of his heart, more of his wealth, or more of his intellect and power, such as they may be, for the good of this Dominion of Canada." It was an electrifying finale, but they were the words of a beaten politician.

Four days later, Alexander Campbell complained that "had Sir John A[.] kept straight during the last fortnight, the Ministry would not have been defeated." Dufferin regarded Macdonald's "physical infirmity" as "a source of intolerable embarrassment at every turn, for unfortunately it is when affairs are at a crisis that it overtakes him." But the alcohol problem was only a symptom. Fundamentally, the crisis stemmed from Macdonald's failure to win a strong majority in 1872. He had hoped that the six recently arrived MPs from Prince Edward Island, Canada's newest province, would support the government that now ruled their destinies. The Islanders reviewed the political situation — and four of them joined the opposition. On November 4, the influential Manitoba MP Donald A. Smith sought an interview. Smith had proved a wise negotiator during the Red River troubles, but Macdonald disliked him and agreed to the meeting reluctantly. After twenty minutes, Smith stalked out, complaining that Macdonald had "done nothing but curse and swear at me." Smith "ratted" that evening. Next day, November 5, 1873, the government resigned, with Macdonald putting his characteristic "spin" on the disaster that most believed would end his career. "I have long yearned for rest and am not sorry to have it forced on me," he assured Gowan. "I believe Canada will do me justice in the long run." As Alexander Mackenzie formed the new government, Liberal MPs celebrated by singing their own version of *Clementine*: "Sir John is dead and gone for ever." But was he?

The five years that John A. Macdonald spent in opposition are dismissed by his admirers as a blip that the voters corrected after enduring the inadequate Mackenzie Liberals. In fact, that period divided into three phases. The first, one of wild and ill-advised activity, crashed after four months with a Conservative rout in a snap general election. The second, from 1874 to 1876, plunged Macdonald's life into its deepest trough. The third saw him solve both personal and political challenges, overcoming his alcohol problem and rebuilding his party to return to office in 1878.

Tactically, Macdonald should have adopted a low profile after his resignation. Mackenzie encountered problems hammering disparate factions into a Cabinet. Luther Holton, the party's finance expert, refused the portfolio, which went to Richard Cartwright, the former Conservative outraged by the appointment of Hincks ("and now you see the company he has got into," sneered Macdonald). Two other prominent Liberals, Edward Blake from Ontario and A.-A. Dorion from Quebec, soon resigned. Mackenzie would have called (and won) an early election anyway, but initially he planned a short parliamentary session to clean up election laws. This would have highlighted the inexperience of the new ministers, only three of whom had previously held political office, two of them very briefly. Renewing his proclaimed opposition strategy of 1862–63, Macdonald promised to "subordinate Party to Country." In reality, he seemed to be planning to repeat the ambush that had destroyed George Brown in 1858. This was a tactical blunder which gave Mackenzie the excuse to go to the polls immediately.

One clue to Macdonald's intentions only surfaced four years later. As prime minister, he had personally administered Canada's secret service fund. With casual arrogance, he omitted to inform Mackenzie that he still controlled its $32,000 balance. By the time Macdonald wound up the fund in 1875, another $6,000 had been disbursed for purposes, as Mackenzie grumbled, "of which he constituted himself the sole judge." Protesting that "not one farthing of the money was ever in my hands," Macdonald insisted he could not name the recipients without endangering them. Hence Ontario Protestants never discovered that the fund had been used to bribe Louis Riel to get out of Manitoba.

Far from radiating dignified humility, Macdonald defiantly accepted a banquet in his honour just one week after his resignation. He was led through the Ottawa streets by a band, playing "When Johnny Comes Marching Home Again." "Can I believe my senses?" he asked the assembled throng. "Am I a defeated man or am I a victorious minister?" Dismissing the Pacific Scandal charges against him as "unjust ... foul and unfair," he predicted that his party would soon return to office, but hoped he would "never be a member of any administration again." He gave contradictory signals. "I cannot last much longer.... But I will remain as long as I can of any service." Conservatives would find younger leaders, whom "you will be proud to follow with the same constancy as you have followed me." In an era before party conventions and mass memberships, it is hard to see how this new leadership could emerge, especially while Macdonald remained in place. The shell-shocked caucus had re-elected him as leader: nobody else wanted the job.

Mackenzie's new ministers faced the usual by-elections, and most were returned by acclamation. But Macdonald denounced the "ingratitude, and base treachery" of his former acolyte, Cartwright. Insultingly, the new finance minister sent Macdonald a forty dollar cheque for travelling expenses so that they could debate face to face: Macdonald, of course, never cashed it. At the ensuing confrontation, Cartwright, who was handily re-elected, tried to goad Macdonald into punching him as he had assaulted Carruthers at Kingston. A second by-election resulted from a last-minute Macdonald patronage appointment, which opened the strong Tory riding of West Toronto. Just before Christmas 1873, the 1,043 to 574 Conservative majority of 1872 was turned around into a 1,577 to 1,066 Liberal triumph.

Now confident of victory, Mackenzie capitalized on West Toronto to call an immediate general election. In February 1874 the Conservatives were reduced to sixty-seven MPs in the 206-seat House of Commons. In some respects, Macdonald's party did surprisingly well. In Ontario, although thirteen Liberals were returned by acclamation, the Conservatives polled almost half the votes across the contested ridings, a good base for a comeback. However, they retained only twenty-two seats in the province: Macdonald himself won Kingston by just thirty-eight votes, and was promptly hit by a petition to unseat him for corruption. His own government had tightened election laws so that candidates could be disqualified even if they were conveniently ignorant of corrupt actions by supporters — and the petition alleged seventy-one of them! If barred from representing Kingston, Macdonald would have found it hard to find another riding — and he might even have been disqualified from sitting in Parliament altogether. When the case was heard in November 1873, he attempted damage limitation, acknowledging that "indiscreet" expenditure by his campaign manager, Alexander Campbell, rendered his election invalid. Campbell had prudently decamped to the United States and could not be summoned to give evidence. The manoeuvre saved Macdonald from outright disqualification, but he had to contest Kingston again, scraping in by seventeen votes.

Sir John A. Macdonald's career had now reached his lowest point. Reviewing the political scene in March 1874, Lord Dufferin thought it tragic that Macdonald's "creditable" public service "should have ended in such humiliation." Macdonald himself seemed unsure of his future. "My fighting days are over, I think," he told Tupper. But at about the same time, he gave the journalist N.F. Davin a lively sketch of the future transcontinental Canada, adding "in his own emphatic way," "That is the time when I should like to lead."

During 1874–75, the disorganized Conservatives barely offered any opposition in the House of Commons — although they used their Senate numbers to block Mackenzie's railway deal with the irate British Columbians. Macdonald was refocusing his life away from Ottawa. He had already moved his law practice to Toronto, the main office of its principal client, the Trust and Loan Company. In September 1874 he decided to work there himself, although he kept secret that "I intend to fix my Habitat away from Kingston" until he had won his by-election. "I had to go to work at my trade and earn my living in Toronto," he recalled a decade later.

Macdonald's son Hugh had joined the firm, but the opportunity to reunite the family went badly wrong. A likeable young man, Hugh urged his father in 1874 to leave the bulk of his property to his handicapped half-sister Mary, "simply giving me a trifle to show that I have not been cut off for bad behaviour." But father and son soon quarrelled over Hugh's plans to marry — probably because his bride was a Catholic. Protesting that Macdonald was "unnecessarily harsh," Hugh struck out on his own although, characteristically, he insisted that he could "never forget the numbers of kindnesses done and favours conferred upon me in times past." Happily, the breach was soon healed.

The move to practising law in Toronto confirmed the impression that Macdonald was only a caretaker leader, waiting for a replacement to appear. But when he was challenged, in September 1875, he refused to disappear. Announcing that Macdonald's re-election as party leader had been a "grave mistake," Alexander Galt offered to lead a new party. It was a typically inept move by an impulsive personality. Galt had not mobilized any supporters: indeed, he was not even in Parliament at the time. Macdonald easily brushed aside the challenge. The humiliated Galt soon begged to resume friendly relations. "The wound may be considered as healed over," Macdonald stiffly replied, "but the scar will ... remain for some time." A second by-election in West Toronto (whose Liberal MP had become a judge) in November 1875 returned the riding to

Courtesy of Topley Studio/Library and Archives Canada/PA-025352.

Macdonald's son, Hugh John, 1871. He survived a haphazard upbringing and a quarrel with his father to become a Winnipeg lawyer.

its natural allegiance. Macdonald then delivered a fiery speech in Montreal, proving himself still the undisputed leader of the Conservative party, even if it was going nowhere. In June 1877, he announced that he would hold the job "until my friends say that I have served long enough." He even nominated the abrasive Tupper as his successor, thereby ensuring that nobody would ask him to go.

One problem in Macdonald's life remained as serious as ever: he was drinking too much and too often. "If ever there was a man in low water," the journalist W.F. Maclean recalled, "it was Sir John as I saw him one day in the winter of 1875." He watched Macdonald "tottering" down Parliament Hill, "others passing him with a wide sweep." There was an embarrassing episode in the House of Commons one February evening that year: the *Mail's* Ottawa correspondent attempted "to veil the facts" in his report, but Macdonald's "condition was well known." Mackenzie deplored Macdonald's "vehement language" and there was "intense anger" among Conservative MPs. A few days later, Mackenzie dismissed another late-night tirade with the comment that Macdonald "appeared to be speaking under some unusual excitement." In 1876, while on a speaking tour of western Ontario with Charles Tupper, he stayed at Patteson's hobby farm near Ingersoll. "Sir John got very drunk at dinner" and insulted Tupper, driving Agnes to walk out in protest. "She had a good deal to put up with," Patteson recalled.

There are many legends of "John A. drunk" but, by definition, "John A. beating the bottle" generated few anecdotes. Yet, in the mid-1870s, Macdonald overcame his alcohol problem. In May 1877, Lord Dufferin noted that he "could drink wine at dinner without being tempted to excess, which hitherto he has never been able to do." Macdonald survived the 1877 session without a single binge. In 1878, when he fell asleep during an all-night debate, Conservative MPs queued up to denounce the *Globe's* allegation that he was "drunk in the plain ordinary sense of that word" — denials they had never dared offer before. Joseph Pope, Macdonald's secretary from 1883, insisted that the problem was resolved "long before I knew him." In 1884, a British statesman called Macdonald "a singular instance of a successful man of great ability and industry who is subject to fits of drunkenness" but added: "I believe he has been more sober lately." Shattered by grief at her mother's death in 1875, Agnes had persuaded Macdonald to join the Anglican Church, another landmark in distancing himself from his Scottish heritage. However, it was digestion, not religion, which triggered reformation. Macdonald told Dufferin that "his constitution has quite changed of late," implying that his metabolism could no longer cope with alcohol. Had he failed to tackle the problem, Macdonald could hardly have achieved another dozen years as Canada's prime minister.

In 1876, almost by accident, the Conservative party found both the new policy and the fresh organizational base needed to win elections. Coming into office in 1873, the Liberals were doubly unlucky: the high-spending Macdonald government bequeathed them a deficit and the world economy took a downturn. The Mackenzie years became associated with gloomy recession, and Macdonald was tempted to adopt a magic-wand policy to get the country moving again. The inspiring idea, called the National Policy, was tariff protection, using duties on imports to create jobs in Canada. Its adoption as a key party plank meant rejecting an intellectual consensus, imported from Britain, in favour of free trade. As the world's leading industrial power, the British preached the virtues of the level playing field, importing food and raw materials duty-free, or imposing low tariffs that made no distinction by country of origin. In Britain, free trade had become what we now call "politically correct": it was not only stupid but wicked to support protection — and British intellectual hegemony dominated Canadian discourse. Free trade, Macdonald complained in 1876, had become not just a religion but a superstition: Liberal contributions to economic debate consisted of "long quotations from political economists."

However beautiful free trade theory, it did not fit Canadian circumstances. Four million Canadians lived alongside forty million Americans, who ruthlessly used tariffs to develop their own industries. In 1874, George Brown, Mackenzie's special envoy, negotiated a draft Reciprocity Treaty in Washington, to replace the agreement the Americans had killed in 1866. The pact provided for cross-border free trade in both natural products and manufactures, but the U.S. Senate contemptuously refused even to put it to the vote. As the continental recession set in, American manufacturers treated Canada as a "sacrifice" or "slaughter" market, dumping their overstocks at cheap prices, sacrificing their profits but slaughtering their Canadian competitors. As Macdonald said in 1876, "we have played that conciliatory game long enough": Canadians should treat Americans "as they treat us."

There was a second reason why, as Macdonald had argued as far back as 1860, it was "useless to discuss the abstract principles of Free Trade and Protection" in Canada. Britain had a broad revenue base, raising government cash from goods and services taxes and income tax. These were abominations to Canadians: they only succumbed to income tax under wartime pressure in 1917, while potential revenue-raising areas such as tavern licences belonged to the provinces. Hence the Dominion derived about sixty percent of its income from import duties — double the proportion in Britain. "We must trust to our customs, therefore, as the principal source of our future revenue," Macdonald stated in 1876. Britain could afford free trade; Canada could not.

Canada's over-reliance upon import duties caused problems in funding the government when trade fell off. In 1874, Finance Minister Cartwright raised the overall tariff to 17.5 percent, so that anybody importing $100 of foreign goods paid $117.50 for them. But, as doctrinaire free traders, the Liberals refused to vary the rates to help Canadian producers. However, back in 1858, Macdonald's provincial ministry had experimented with a different approach. As he explained, "we took off the duties on the necessaries of life which the poor man uses … we increased those on articles of luxury, which the rich man buys" and "we raised the taxation on those goods which our own mechanics can manufacture … to give them incidental protection." "Incidental protection" became a coded term: free trade might be best in theory but, since Canada had to operate a revenue tariff, it should be tweaked to help Canadian producers.

The 1876 budget proved the turning point. Cartwright surprised Parliament by leaving the tariff unchanged. When the debate began, Macdonald refused to discuss "the merits of protection and free trade." However, one week later, he declared that Canada should "so adjust our tariff for revenue purposes … to develop our resources, the duties falling upon the articles we ourselves are capable of producing." Mackenzie sarcastically congratulated him on finding "a resting place which he may call a policy." If everybody was to be protected, Mackenzie argued, nobody would gain. "If, on the other hand, only certain classes are to be protected, I want to know what the classes are."

Of course, Macdonald, the skilled political operator, responded by hinting to every interest group that their products would receive protection, while their essential supplies would be imported duty-free. New Brunswicker Peter Mitchell ran in the 1878 election on the assurance that a Conservative government would impose no tariff on flour, a vital commodity in a timber province that grew very little of its own food. In mid-campaign, news broke that Macdonald had promised Ontario millers that he would tax American flour, and Mitchell lost his election. "I couldn't help it," Macdonald pleaded. "I was sincere when I told you what I did." In a catch-all formula, the Conservatives offered "a judicious readjustment of the tariff" to "foster the agricultural, the mining, the manufacturing and other interests of the Dominion," prevent emigration, restore prosperity, and force the Americans to grant Reciprocity. Sir John A. was expert at making people believe he would deliver what they wanted. As Lord Dufferin noted, Macdonald charmed politicians from Canada's discontented Pacific province with promises that under the Conservatives, "every man in British Columbia should have a branch railway at his own door."

Macdonald wrapped the transcontinental railway into the National Policy package: the railway would fill the West with settlers, who would become customers for central Canadian factories. He nicknamed it "N.P." — sometimes whimsically interpreted as "no poverty" or "new potatoes" — arguing that it would build a cross-class alliance of factory workers, farmers, and capitalists. Macdonald had targeted working men since 1872, when newspaperman George Brown had reacted to the formation of a printers' union by having its leaders imprisoned for conspiracy. Finance Minister Cartwright insisted that Canadians must "atone" for previous extravagance by "thrift and hard work;" Macdonald offered them hope. Cartwright warned that the recession was "no time for experiments"; Macdonald poked fun at "a Reform Government with nothing to reform."

Macdonald's almost accidental adoption of protection was followed by the equally fortuitous discovery of a new form of political campaigning. On July 1, 1876, he addressed hundreds

Macdonald looks sad as he faces the 1878 election. Was his career a failure?

of Dominion Day vacationers at a picnic at Uxbridge, sixty kilometres northeast of Toronto. A massive success, the picnic was the first in a series of outdoor extravaganzas through the summer months of 1876 and 1877, held across Ontario and even into the English-speaking Eastern Townships of Quebec. Privately, he called them "infernal things," but they contributed powerfully to the John A. Macdonald legend. Unlike political meetings, which were generally all-male and potentially rowdy, picnics were family occasions for fun, friendship, and flirtation. In this benign environment, Macdonald mobilized his famous charm, shrugging off the Pacific Scandal with the plaintive protest that "he had worked for thirty years, and yet had not amassed wealth." He exploited the presence of women, assuring the farmer's wife that protection would help her sell eggs from her henhouse in the factory towns which, like those railways in British Columbia, would spring up in everybody's neighbourhood.

His magic touch as a speaker was captured by one observer, writing in 1883 after Macdonald had returned to office. "Sometimes, by a familiar word or two, you see him levelling distinctions between himself and the audience." As a result, all those present — farmers, labourers, tradesmen — "feel that they and the prime-minister are assembled there on a common mission — the prime-minister only happens to *be* prime minister, and speaking then; anyone else, also, might have been." Yet gradually, the crowd realized "that the speaker is the man who is doing their work the best." Macdonald broke down barriers between himself and his hearers: "the *I* is lost in the *we*." In 1876–77, when it still seemed unlikely that he would return to office, he varied the theme, praising audiences for their disinterested support for a politician who might never reward them. "How was it, he sometimes asked himself, that he without means, power or patronage … should be so received?" he mused, praising the "British fair play" of Brockville picnickers in 1877.

Macdonald's critics claimed that he built up support networks by handing out jobs, and he was certainly ruthless in manipulating expectations of patronage, which often remained unfulfilled. But he could never have amassed the 133,633 votes he won across Ontario in 1878, and the still larger number in the rest of Canada, purely by dangling individual favours. If anything, the reverse was true: Macdonald inspired fervent support among people who felt nobly patriotic simply because they idolized "John A." "There was nothing that his followers would not do or suffer for him," and this devotion was "strong among those who had never even seen him." But, in their turn, those dedicated and high-minded supporters felt entitled to rebuke and correct their leader for his human failings. "It is not because you are deemed faultless that this large Assembly has met to do you honour," Macdonald was told at Simcoe in 1876. Modern spin-doctors would be horrified at riding officials telling their leader that "if you erred in the administration of affairs your errors were of judgment and not of intention." However, Macdonald humbly accepted the reprimand, confessing to "acts of omission and commission which I regret" but consoling himself that his supporters accepted that "I was acting … for the interest of our common country." Most politicians are judged by their deeds rather than their intentions: John A. Macdonald led a charmed life as a special exception.

Reviewing the political scene at the close of 1877, the *Montreal Gazette* noted that the picnics had raised Macdonald's popularity to levels "few people could have anticipated," and predicted that he would "sweep the country" at the upcoming general election. The claim, even from a friendly newspaper, would hardly have been credible two years earlier. One Conservative supporter who had mixed feelings about the come-back was the leader's wife, who had spent the past two years home-making in Toronto. Agnes had to tread carefully. "My lord and master ... simply lives to please and gratify me" at home, but Macdonald was "*absolutely* tyrannical in his public life," snubbing her if she commented on political matters. In July 1878, she plucked up courage to ask whether the forthcoming election would take them back to Ottawa. "If we do well, we shall have a majority of sixty," he replied; "if badly, forty."

Canadians voted on September 17, 1878. On election night, veteran Liberal Luther Holton watched as telegrams flooded into a Montreal newsroom announcing a Conservative sweep — not by forty, nor sixty, but a majority of eighty seats. Eventually, Holton broke his silence with the comment: "Well! John A. beats the devil." Macdonald had certainly vanquished two personal demons: he had overcome his alcohol problem, and his election victory drew a line under the humiliating Pacific Scandal. One setback clouded the victory: after thirty-three years as their MP, Macdonald was rejected in Kingston as the "Do-Nothing Deserter" who had moved to Toronto. He was quickly elected as absentee member for Victoria in British Columbia. Campbell consoled him, "if you were defeated in Kingston, you have been elected by the Dominion."

7

1878–1886
The Realization of All My Dreams

When Canada's first prime minister died in 1891, a sorrowing colleague claimed that the history of Canada for the previous fifty years was "the life of Sir John Macdonald." That was an exaggeration, but during his final term as prime minister, Macdonald's life and Canada's history were closely entwined — perhaps too closely. The completion of the Canadian Pacific Railway in 1885 should have crowned his career, but the triumph was marred by Louis Riel's Western uprising that same year. Far from departing the scene in triumph, he would spend the last five years of his life fire-fighting a series of threats, most of them knock-on problems from the crisis of 1885.

Macdonald's National Policy introduced a firm political dividing line, making it harder for "loose fish" to switch parties — although one Quebec senator jumped to the Liberals, complaining at Macdonald's inability to speak French. However, Western demands for inclusion in the system, coupled with the overwhelming financial needs of the railway, forced representatives of the older provinces into defensive blocks: at crucial moments, Macdonald was held to ransom by his own supporters. In many respects, he remained the Ontario leader, dealing with other provinces through allies rather than subordinates. As late as 1878, Macdonald had never visited New Brunswick, and he did not travel west of Lake Huron until 1886. Negotiations to recruit the Halifax lawyer John Thompson to Cabinet in 1885 were conducted through his Nova Scotian colleagues. The prime minister's first direct approach began: "I am of course aware that you have been asked to join our ministry." Careful negotiations were required to secure the "cordial assent" of existing ministers to the appointment of Thomas White in 1885 — necessary, Macdonald assured him, because the fifty-four-year-old White would "be a Minister long after I am off the stage." Sadly, White died of overwork three years later. Above all, Macdonald had no control over Quebec, where his lieutenant, Hector Langevin, was constantly undermined by party rivals.

The "Old Man" preferred to work with associates he had known for years: it took seven years for any MP from the 1878 intake to make it into Cabinet. Initially, he based his team on two stalwarts, Tilley as finance minister to launch the National Policy, Tupper to drive the Pacific Railway project. But Tilley was exhausted by 1885, while from 1883 Tupper preferred the post of High Commissioner in London, although he remained semi-involved in domestic politics. David Macpherson had helped rear Macdonald's son during Isabella's illness in 1856: Macdonald put him in charge of the West in 1883. The prime minister was deeply attached to John Henry Pope, the loyal, gruff Anglo-Quebecker who once dismissed three Cabinet colleagues as "smaller than the little end of nothing." Macdonald first met him in 1849; they had

Macdonald liked to disguise his age by wearing light-coloured suits.

been parliamentary colleagues since 1857. When "John Henry" (who was not related to the prime minister's secretary, "Joe" Pope) worked himself to death in 1889, Macdonald broke down making the announcement to the Commons.

Ministerial talent was thin among MPs. Thompson was imported because there was an "equality of unfitness" among Nova Scotian Conservative backbenchers. In 1880, Macdonald decided to placate New Brunswick politician John Costigan, by promoting his son, a post office clerk in Winnipeg. "We can't make him a Cabinet minister (which he wants) & must help the son." In fact, Costigan gained his objective in 1882, although an alcohol problem limited his usefulness. Both Costigan and another Irish Catholic, Frank Smith, threatened resignation over patronage issues, and Macdonald dared not call their bluff. He had blocked one of Tupper's appointments in 1879, and for two years his Nova Scotian colleague refused to speak to him. Appointed a minister in 1882, Joseph-Adolphe Chapleau proved greedy for patronage. Macdonald felt that he was "comparatively *harmless*" inside Cabinet, a theory shattered during the 1887 election when Chapleau threatened to bolt the campaign unless given exclusive control over government appointments in the Montreal area. The prime minister surrendered. When Pope's death vacated the Railways portfolio, with its massive patronage, Chapleau was "crazy to get it." Macdonald dared not offend the Quebecker by appointing a rival, so he took the job himself — an absurd addition to the workload of a seventy-four-year-old prime minister. Macdonald tried to persuade one of his ablest Ontario supporters to join the Cabinet: D'Alton McCarthy was a fine debater and effective campaigner. But McCarthy refused to leave his lucrative law practice for what Macdonald admitted was "the thankless & inglorious position of a Canadian Minister." The appointment, in 1888, of the thirty-two-year-old Charles Hibbert Tupper was a gesture to his father, whose faults he energetically magnified. The prime minister returned one of his importunate letters with the scribbled advice: "skin your own skunks." Even Sir John A. Macdonald had difficulty managing this disparate team. As the years passed, it became steadily harder to imagine anybody replacing him.

Macdonald offered simple advice to these who feared that the 1879 tariff would make imported foodstuffs more expensive: "use no American flour ... but eat Canadian flour, on which there was no tax." He invariably linked the tariff to the construction of the transcontinental railway: when Western settlers complained that Canadian goods were more expensive, he sarcastically offered them "the glorious privilege" of importing American manufactures duty-free — so long as they could be transported by toboggan. Linking tariff and railway made political sense in Canada, but it caused problems in Britain. The Pacific Railway needed British investment capital, but British manufacturers objected to Canadian import duties — after all, their taxes paid for the navy that defended Canada. Hence Macdonald visited Britain in 1879 and 1880, defending the National Policy to politicians and angry businessmen.

Crossing the Atlantic in 1879 enabled Macdonald to accept membership of Britain's Privy Council, a political Hall of Fame dating from the sixteenth century. The distinction had been offered after the Treaty of Washington, but with a hint not to collect it until the Pacific Scandal died down. Sworn in by Queen Victoria, Macdonald became the first "Right Honourable" colonist in the overseas Empire. Britain's veteran prime minister, Benjamin Disraeli, invited "the Canadian chief" to an overnight stopover at his country house. Disraeli found his visitor "gentlemanlike, agreeable, and very intelligent, a considerable man," noting with approval "no Yankeeisms" in his speech, "except a little sing-song occasionally at the end of a sentence." Soon after, Macdonald assured Disraeli of Canada's "pleasurable excitement" at actually being mentioned in one of his speeches.

This cloying sentiment disguised a nationalist agenda. Macdonald dismissed people who argued for Canadian independence as "fools": standing alone, the Dominion would be overwhelmed by the Americans. But he wanted to move towards partnership with Britain. He talked freely with a British royal commission on defence issues in 1880, predicting that Canada would raise its own small army to share imperial responsibilities, although his insistence upon strict confidentiality kept his evidence secret for seventy years. Macdonald also persuaded the reluctant British government to accept an official Canadian representative in London: he urged the title "Resident Minister" but the imperial authorities preferred the vaguer term "High Commissioner" — an office held first by Galt and then by Tupper. But Macdonald made no commitment to shed Canadian blood in imperial wars: when Britain entangled itself in Sudan in 1885, he flatly refused to help.

As in 1872, the government wished the Pacific Railway to be built by a heavily-subsidized private company. In 1880, Macdonald chose a syndicate headed by Montreal banker George Stephen. At first, this seemed an odd choice, for Stephen was running a north-south railway linking Winnipeg to the United States — while Macdonald's aim was an all-Canadian, east-west route. However, Stephen had profited from his Minnesota project through selling railroad land grants to settlers, and he saw the potential of similarly developing the Canadian West. Stephen came to depend upon Macdonald's personal support, further obligating the prime minister to stay in office. Relations with Stephen's business partner, Donald Smith, were less easy: Smith had deserted the government in 1873 and, five years later, Macdonald had denounced him as "the biggest liar I ever met!" But Macdonald believed that politicians "cannot afford to be governed by any feeling of irritation and annoyance," and eventually the two men buried their hatchet. The Canadian Pacific Railway company (CPR) was launched in 1880, with a promised subsidy of $25 million and twenty-five million acres (10.11 million hectares) of land.

By 1880, Canada was likely to build some form of railway to the Pacific. Even the unenthusiastic Liberal government, with its pessimistic, piecemeal policy, had constructed one section from Lake Superior towards Manitoba, and another in mainland British Columbia. As Macdonald commented, since Mackenzie had built "two ends of a railway, we must finish the middle." But he was determined that the line must also run north of Lake Superior, giving central Canada a direct link to the prairies. If the transcontinental railway began at Thunder Bay, it would be accessible by Great Lakes shipping only in summer. "But for you," Stephen wrote Macdonald in 1884, the railway would have been "simply an extension" of the American railroads in winter, "in short, not a *Canadian* Pacific Railway at all." But Stephen's price for tackling the unpromising Canadian Shield was CPR control over all prairie branch lines southward from the main line. Unless the Americans could be prevented from siphoning off its traffic, nobody "would give one dollar for the whole line east of Winnipeg." This CPR monopoly was unpopular in Manitoba.

Macdonald was sixty-five in 1880, and running the government was a tough job. His overseas trip the previous summer had been delayed by severe sickness, with "cramps and spasms" that reminded him of the 1870 gallstones crisis. Macdonald was ill again in March 1880, and horrified his colleagues by talking about retirement. In April 1881, he asked Campbell to prepare documentation about British Columbia: "I intended to have done it myself but I am not up to the work." Soon after, he collapsed: "strength gone and troubled with continued pain in the stomach and bowels," he reported to Tupper. His Ottawa doctor suspected cancer and advised "that I had better put my affairs in order." His sister Louisa was shocked by her brother's appearance. "I never saw John looking what I would call old until this time." For the third time in two years, he crossed the Atlantic, this time to seek medical advice. A London specialist pronounced him "free from organic disease" but insisted upon "a very rigid diet & complete rest." (Macdonald was now seen as such an asset to the Empire that the doctor refused to charge a fee.) "I am slowly getting better but my strength does not return as I could wish," he told Campbell in June 1881.

Nonetheless, he yearned to be back at his desk: "I have no pleasure nowadays but in work, & so it will be to the end of the chapter." The chapter was never-ending, especially because the Pacific Railway and the development of Canadian industries were both long-term projects. It was vital to win another term in government and Macdonald's "remaining ambition is to see that our policy is not reversed." But to ensure that that the National Policy would be "safe from 1883 to 1888," voters had to be persuaded that it was working. "You cannot plant the seed to-day and get the crop to-morrow," he warned. Fortunately, times were good and, in 1882, he called an early election.

Although the Mowat Liberal government remained firmly entrenched in Ontario, Macdonald had a temporary advantage on his chief battleground by the early 1880s. After a quarter century of arrogant dominance, the *Globe* was under pressure. Although the Toronto *Mail* had struggled, Macdonald "actually wept" when he lost control over it to its creditors in 1877. However, his luck rebounded: run on business lines, the *Mail* soon rivalled the *Globe* in circulation and, until 1885, preached Conservative policies. Financially, too, the *Globe* was under challenge from an evening paper founded in 1876, the Toronto *Telegram*, which aggressively marketed want-ads and cut into the *Globe's* advertising revenue. George Brown responded in 1880 with an expensive re-launch — at just the moment when a disgruntled ex-employee shot him. Brown died six weeks later. "I do not often read the *Globe*," Macdonald remarked in 1882. It remained as hostile to him as ever, but it was a greatly reduced threat.

The 1881 census showed that Ontario was entitled to four additional parliamentary seats. Next year, in an episode nicknamed "Hiving the Grits," Macdonald proposed extensive boundary changes right across the province. The original plan was to confine a small number of opposition MPs within overwhelmingly Liberal ridings, while a larger number of Conservatives would be elected by smaller majorities. However, the redistribution was modified when Macdonald's backbenchers panicked at this high-risk strategy, and its overall effect is hard to assess. Essentially, the Liberals lost in Ontario in 1882 for the classic reason that they failed to win enough votes. The Conservatives outpolled them by 3,700 votes, just 1.4 percent, enough to net them a fifty-five to thirty-seven seat plurality. As Macdonald later joked, his boundary changes were a "gerrymander," but Mowat's redrawing of the provincial electoral map was a "readjustment": in 1879, the provincial Liberals had won the Ontario election by less than 2,000 votes — 0.8 percent — which translated into a fifty-seven to thirty-one seat victory. "We meant to make you howl," Macdonald allegedly told one of the Liberals who lost his seat, but his motive was strategic not sadistic: by protesting, his opponents likely talked themselves into losing. As usual, the Ontario Liberals forgot the rest of Canada, which cumulatively re-elected the Conservatives by 139 seats to seventy-one. Macdonald's election for Lennox, his childhood home, was overturned for irregularities, and he represented Carleton, in the Ottawa hinterland. He felt "used up" by the "hard fight" across the province. But in Berlin (later Kitchener), seven-year-old Willy King watched the prime minister receiving a bouquet from a pretty girl and concluded that "politics had its rewards." As William Lyon Mackenzie King, he would become the only Canadian leader to serve for longer than Macdonald himself.

Unwisely, Sir John A. Macdonald assured Parliament in 1883 that "not one single farthing of the cost of building the railway should fall on the older Provinces." This was a reckless boast, since Stephen had already warned him that the railway was "going to cost a great deal more money than we calculated on." Raising cash proved increasingly difficult. Far from reassuring investors, the government's decision, in October 1883, to guarantee the CPR's annual dividend only highlighted the project's financial problems. On December 15, a desperate Stephen told Macdonald that there was "no way on God's earth" that the Canadian Pacific could escape bankruptcy without a massive loan from the government. Legend claims that Macdonald told a late-night CPR delegation that they might as well ask him for the planet Jupiter: Cabinet and Parliament would never agree. He was roused at 2:00 a.m. by John Henry Pope with a blunt warning: if the Canadian Pacific collapsed, the Conservative party would follow within twenty-four hours. The story, told years later, is probably a conflation of different episodes, since

Stephen thanked Macdonald "for the readiness which you have shown throughout to help us in every possible way." The prime minister now had to persuade his own followers that the Canadian Pacific was going to cost another $22.5 million — roughly Ottawa's annual revenue. Officially, it was a loan, but the security was the Railway itself. Parliament approved in March 1884, but Quebec Conservatives ostentatiously absented themselves during the debates. The price of their support was funding for the North Shore Railway, connecting Montreal and Quebec City but through thinly populated country north of the St. Lawrence. Maritimers demanded construction of the Short Line, a direct link to Montreal through northern Maine. The Canadian Pacific had run out of cash and Sir John A. Macdonald was exhausting his political capital.

"I bore the strain wonderfully well," Macdonald told Gowan at the close of the "tedious & disagreeable session," but he conceded that "it *was* a strain greater than I should like to encounter again." To Campbell, he was more open. "My daily exhaustion is very great, although not so perceptible to others as to myself." "I would leave the Government tomorrow," he told Tupper, but for the fear that "Stephen would throw up the sponge if I did." A summer break down the St. Lawrence was followed by a voyage to England, where his London specialist found "no flaw" in his basic health, attributing his indigestion to "work & worry." The British elite welcomed Macdonald like a friendly potentate. He spoke for an hour at a banquet in his honour, a speech that one diner thought "would have been a very good one if it had been a little more condensed." Queen Victoria invited him to stay overnight at Windsor Castle, and thought him "an interesting, agreeable old man." He returned home to a massive demonstration in Toronto to mark his forty years in politics, followed — in January 1885 — by a celebration of his seventieth birthday in Montreal. Of course, the adulation could not continue.

It was not that the government had no warning of trouble in the West, but rather that too much alarming noise came from that troubled region. Although treaties had been signed with native people to extinguish Aboriginal title across the prairies by 1877, the "Indians" (as Native people were generally

"Seedy looking old beggar, isn't he?" commented a supporter in 1886.

called) remained a source of concern. Macdonald uttered worthy sentiments. "The Indians are the aborigines — the original occupants of the country, and their rights must be respected." But he distrusted "any philanthropic idea of protecting the Indian" especially by preserving "semi-savage customs." "The whole thing is a question of management," he pronounced, and "management" meant keeping Aboriginal communities quiet while settlers took over the West.

The influx of settlers into Manitoba had pushed many Métis to follow the dwindling buffalo herds to the North Saskatchewan valley. Under the 1870 deal, male heads of Métis families had been granted "scrip," vouchers for free land grants. Some claimed they had never received their entitlement, others demanded a fresh handout. Unsympathetic, Macdonald claimed many Métis had sold out to speculators. In any case, they could obtain free land grants of 160 acres (about sixty-five hectares) under Canada's homestead policy to encourage settlers. Throughout 1884, Ottawa was more concerned with hotheads in the Manitoba Farmers' Protective Union: Macdonald's son Hugh, now a lawyer in Winnipeg, warned they might seize unguarded militia stores if an insurrection broke out. It seemed implausible that the Métis would take action on their own, but they might get caught up in some wider movement. In September 1884, there were reports of possible trouble around Battleford. "I don't attach much importance to these rumours," Macdonald wrote, "but there is no harm in taking precautions."

Louis Riel had returned from the United States in July 1884. Macdonald intended "to deal liberally" with Riel and use him to "keep the Métis in order." The governor general, Lord Lansdowne, agreed that Riel's reappearance was "anything but a misfortune." Unfortunately, continuing anger in Ontario at the killing of Thomas Scott made direct negotiations with Riel politically impossible and, as in 1869–70, he proved difficult to pin down through intermediaries: terms submitted in September were described as "what we request for the present." Riel also conflated Métis grievances with personal compensation claims, imaginatively estimated at $100,000, making the mistake of seemingly presenting them as a blackmailer's price to quit Canada. Paying Riel to disappear, Macdonald insisted, would be an admission of government weakness. Riel's mental state was a further complication. During 1884–85, he renamed the days of the week and the stars in the sky, declared himself to be a prophet as well as a member of the French royal family, and appointed the archbishop of Montreal as pope of the New World. The government's subsequent claim that Riel's delusions were compatible with rational political action was controversial at the time and unconvincing now.

In December 1884, the Métis dispatched a petition of grievances to Ottawa and, on January 28, 1885, Cabinet authorized an investigation. Macdonald's defenders argue that this rapid response removed any pretext for rebellion: he had acted, he later admitted, "with the greatest reluctance" but on the principle, "let us have peace" — the voice of the traumatized veteran of 1837. But critics claim that the angry Métis interpreted the move as a delaying tactic. Government public relations proved poor: Riel was offended to hear the news casually some days later, a discourtesy that probably pushed him towards rebellion. However, Riel's mystical belief in his own destiny fatally handicapped the uprising. In 1869, trouble had begun in November, while the Red River was inaccessibly wrapped in winter; in 1885, Riel defied the government in March, when spring was in sight and militia forces could be deployed against him. Believing his Métis to be divinely chosen, he made little attempt to build alliances with Native people or discontented settlers. He refused to allow his supporters to exploit their knowledge of the terrain and fight a prolonged guerrilla campaign. He did not even sabotage the Canadian Pacific Railway, which quickly brought government forces from eastern Canada.

Maybe Ottawa could have moved faster in response to Métis grievances, but in the early months of 1885, the government faced what seemed a far greater crisis over the transcontinental railway. Although nearing completion, the CPR had yet again run out of cash. With its assets mortgaged to the government, no private investment was likely but, as Macdonald wrote on January 24, "however docile our majority, we dare not ask for another loan." In fact, his backbenchers were far from docile. On March 17, as the company faced catastrophic financial crisis, Macdonald reported "blackmailing all round," with Quebec and Maritime MPs raising their demands. "I wish I were well out of it." After fruitless talks in Ottawa on March 26, George Stephen regretfully accepted that he must declare bankruptcy. But earlier that day, at Duck Lake in the far-off Saskatchewan country, Louis Riel had led his Métis into a clash with the Northwest Mounted Police, killing twelve of them. On March 27, the news reached Ottawa. It looks like the greatest coincidence in Canadian history, making possible the trade-off that confirmed Macdonald's political genius. He would use the CPR to save the West, and the uprising as the opportunity to rescue the company.

Canada's destiny had a close shave during those two crucial days, but the connection between Riel and the railway is less dramatic than it seems. Central Canada was already aware of trouble in the West; the *Montreal Gazette* headlined "The Riel Rebellion" on March 25. The shootout at Duck Lake was not immediately linked to the CPR, for it was assumed that the Mounted Police and the Winnipeg militia could contain the outbreak. In any case, had the company crashed, the transcontinental railway itself would have become the property of the government, as the CPR's chief creditor. Campbell urged that Cabinet should "face the evils which the fall of the company (if it must fall) would undoubtedly entail" rather than lend any more money. If Macdonald performed a political about-face, posing as "guardian of the country rather than the company," Parliament would surely vote the necessary money to finish the project and the Conservative party would sidestep political disaster. Although this seemed unduly optimistic, once MPs grasped that they would have to pay for its construction anyway, they might accept another CPR bailout. Far from the bad news of March 27 producing a miraculous turnaround in attitudes to the CPR, the company was kept on life support through short-term bank loans for several months. Parliament was debating Macdonald's Franchise Bill — denounced by the Liberals as a device to ensure that only Conservatives were added to the voters' lists — and not until mid-June were proposals for financial aid introduced. In vain, Stephen urged "extreme urgency." Macdonald, he concluded had "the best possible intentions" but it seemed "impossible for him to act until the last moment arrives." "Putting off, his old sin," Campbell called it, adding "Macdonald has lost his grasp." But "Old Tomorrow" judged the timing right, and the necessary funding was secured in July 1885. On November 7, the two ends of the transcontinental railway were joined in the mountains of British Columbia.

Nine days after the famous "Last Spike" completed the CPR, a metal bolt was shot back to open the trapdoor under the Regina gallows, and convicted traitor Louis Riel fell to his death. Riel's execution still divides Canadians, and the prime minister bears chief responsibility for the political decision to confirm the death sentence passed upon the rebel leader. "If Riel is convicted he will certainly be executed," Macdonald wrote in June. From a modern perspective, that sounds like the judicial murder of a political opponent. In the contemporary context, we should emphasize that Riel was the only person to die for his role in the uprising — although eight Aboriginal men were also hanged for a specific crime, the killing of settlers at Frog Lake, with dozens of Native people rounded up to witness the grisly mass execution. Memories of the "martyrs" of 1837 lingered in Quebec, and Macdonald knew that widespread repression would create victims and long-term wounds. He even tried to dismiss the uprising as a "mere domestic trouble" which should not "be elevated to the rank of a rebellion," but he ruefully agreed when Lord Lansdowne objected that the episode was more than "a common riot." "We certainly made it assume large proportions in the public eye ... for our own purposes," Macdonald admitted. Punishing Riel made it possible to exercise clemency to his followers without making the government look weak. Most rebels served only short prison sentences.

The jury that convicted Riel also recommended mercy, an implied criticism of the government's failure to tackle Métis grievances. Therefore, in confirming Riel's death sentence, Macdonald was sitting in judgment on himself. There was the further complication of Riel's mental state: if he was mad, could he be held responsible for his actions? At the last minute, the government commissioned three medical reports on Riel's sanity — although Campbell asked how anybody could determine in November whether he had been sane the previous March. Chosen as lead investigator was Michael Lavell, warden of Kingston's penitentiary — an appointment he owed to Macdonald. Lavell was experienced in dealing with mentally disturbed prisoners, but his medical qualifications were in obstetrics. Macdonald gave him precise but narrow instructions, and Lavell duly reported although Riel was an oddball, he had known right from wrong. Yet Riel's continued insistence on accepting responsibility for his actions as he faced the noose surely cast doubt on his sanity. However, only one of the three doctors, the francophone F.-X. Valade, expressed doubts. Valade's report was not only ignored but misleadingly rewritten for subsequent publication.

Macdonald was bombarded with advice. Send Riel to an asylum and Quebec would demand his release. Fail to hang him, and Ontario would punish the Conservatives at the polls. Basically, Ontario demanded Riel's neck for a crime for which he was never tried, the shooting of Thomas Scott. Macdonald assumed that Riel's religious delusions would neutralize sympathy in Catholic Quebec — but any government campaign to publicize them would have strengthened the case for reprieving him as a madman. Quebec ministers believed Riel's execution would soon be forgotten in their province. "The Riel fever will I think die out," Macdonald wrote a month after the hanging. In fact, the "Riel fever" divided Canadians deeply and enduringly.

It was presumably the triumph of the transcontinental railway and not the tragedy of Riel that motivated a Guelph teenager to write to Macdonald on November 18, 1885: "Take the advice of a thirteen year old Tory & *resign*." Aged seventy and with his greatest work completed, surely he should have heeded Robina Stewart's counsel? "I have done my work and can now sing my *Nunc Dimittis*," he wrote, alluding to the Anglican prayer: "Lord, now lettest thy servant depart in peace." But Macdonald had earned a lap of honour, his first and only journey through western Canada. On July 10, 1886, he quietly left Ottawa by special train for a seven-week tour, accompanied by Agnes, his secretary Joseph Pope, a tame journalist, two servants, and a police bodyguard. His wheelchair-bound daughter, Mary, came too: she was left for treatment at Banff's hot springs while her parents travelled on to the Pacific.

At short notice, Conservative activists gathered to hail their chief, and trackside communities organized civic welcomes. A young Tory at Winnipeg's train station broke off cheering to comment to a friend, "Seedy-looking old beggar, isn't he?" After a side trip through the wheatlands of southern Manitoba, "Canada's grand old man" was greeted with "deafening cheers" at Brandon. Looking "fresh and vigorous," Macdonald delivered "a short impromptu speech well seasoned with his native wit." Carberry presented him with a huge sheaf of wheat. Gleichen hosted a meeting with the Blackfoot nation, in recognition of the loyalty shown by Isapo-Muxica (Crowfoot) during the rebellion: the event was staged more to showcase Macdonald as a benign ruler than to engage with Native grievances. At brief stopovers, Agnes enthusiastically worked the crowds, chatting to women and children. At Calgary, which Macdonald predicted would become "a large metropolitan city," she spent several hours at a social event, meeting "all the ladies who desired to have a chat with the cleverest and most popular lady in Canada today." As their train headed through the mountains, Agnes insisted on riding on the cowcatcher. To the alarm of officials and the terror of Joe Pope, Canada's prime minister joined her for a 200-kilometre stretch. Macdonald "said but little at the time," but in 1891 he wrote of his pride at "looking back from the steps of my car upon the Rocky Mountains fringing the eastern sky."

On July 24, the waters of the Pacific Ocean lapped at his feet as he left the train at Port Moody. Then it was on by steamboat to Victoria, where Macdonald was greeted by a band playing "See the Conquering Hero Comes." A torchlight procession escorted him to a long-vanished hotel, which ruthlessly overcharged for his three-week visit. Tired from travelling, he initially discouraged formal events but quickly became a familiar figure sauntering the downtown streets. But Victoria had elected him to Parliament in 1878, and a delayed welcome ceremony in a packed theatre enabled him to express his thanks. He called his journey "the realization of all my dreams." On August 13, Macdonald formally inaugurated Island's railway to Nanaimo, which he also predicted would become a "great city." That evening, they sailed for the mainland, mesmerized by Mount Baker, "radiant in the southern sky, catching and reflecting the light ... after the sun had disappeared below the horizon." New Westminster was disappointed at receiving only an overnight visit, while the mayor of the recently founded city of Vancouver arrived to express his regret that it had burned down six weeks earlier.

Then followed the long journey home, more speeches, even an appearance at a Conservative convention in Winnipeg. As his train headed across northern Ontario on August 31, 1886, somebody realized that his return to Ottawa would coincide with a massive Liberal rally in the capital addressed by provincial premier Oliver Mowat and federal opposition leader Edward Blake. Local Tories were hastily summoned to a welcoming reception, but the *Globe* crowed that it was a poorly attended "side show." Sir John A. Macdonald had returned to the trench warfare of Canadian politics.

8

1886–1891
You'll Never Die, John A.!

If he had quit politics immediately after his return to Ottawa on August 31, 1886, Sir John A. Macdonald would have ended his career on a high note. In Victoria, he had called the completion of the transcontinental railway "the fruition of all my expectations": surely he was now entitled to bow out? Four years earlier, when a friendly heckler had shouted, "I hope you will never get old," he had modestly replied, "I must make way for others." In 1886 he was seventy-one — high time to act on his promise to "make way for younger and stronger men." Ideally, the fall of 1886 would have seen an orderly transition to a new leader who could meet Parliament that winter and seek a fresh electoral mandate soon after.

It did not happen, and it was never likely. Far from announcing his retirement, Macdonald was planning his thirteenth general election. The central theme of the last five years of his life was his inability to leave public life. His Dominion was like a house with a smouldering basement fire: smoke and flames erupted in room after room, province after province. There would be no second trip to British Columbia, no more comfortable visits to Britain. Far from being confident of Canada's future, he felt foreboding. "We have watched the cradle of Confederation," he had remarked to Campbell the previous year, "& shouldn't like to follow the hearse." Only one possible nation-building target remained. As Gowan commented in 1888, bringing Newfoundland into Confederation "would be a grand capping stone to your original conception and a glorious close to your career in public life." But Macdonald was not inspired by the prospect. "Newfoundland will not come in just now," he replied in September 1888, "and I am not very sorry." Sir John A. Macdonald holds the record as Canada's oldest serving prime minister — a record unlikely to be broken. But his achievement also represented systemic failure: even in his seventies, with his main work achieved, he could not escape from the burden of leadership.

Rejecting Macdonald's 1867 vision of Dominion supremacy over submissive provinces, Mowat's Ontario government had challenged Ottawa in a series of cases before the Judicial Committee of the Privy Council, Canada's ultimate constitutional court. In 1883, a battle over the billiard table in Archibald Hodge's Toronto tavern had prompted the London judges to declare that provinces were "supreme" within their own spheres of jurisdiction. Even Macdonald now occasionally used the term "Federal Government" instead of "Dominion." Although he was astutely aware of "the opposition cry that we are centralizing everything," he remained determined to "protect the Constitution from invasion" by resisting "unworthy concession" to provincial demands. But Mowat had made Ontario a semi-sovereign body within Canada. Worse still, in Nova Scotia, the

Liberals won the 1886 election by threatening to secede from the Dominion altogether.

Macdonald's problems were exacerbated by the Riel case. Defying Conservative policy, the Toronto *Mail* embarked on an anti-French and anti-Catholic campaign which threw the Irish vote to Mowat in the December 1886 Ontario election. The following year, Macdonald launched yet another Toronto newspaper, the *Empire*, but with limited success. Riel's ghost also contributed to a major setback in Quebec, the election of a nationalist Liberal government, led by the unscrupulous adventurer Honoré Mercier.

Conservative defeats in the two largest provinces were an unlikely prelude to a successful Dominion campaign. A cautious politician would have waited until later in 1887: Macdonald defiantly sent Canadians to the polls in February. He knew he was criticized for being "too bold – but boldness won the day." Macdonald gambled that Ontario voters distrusted Mercier and would back a strong leader in Ottawa. The 1885 Franchise Act had created separate Dominion and provincial voter qualifications: Mowat's 1886 provincial victory — narrow enough in the popular vote — was no longer a pointer to the outcome of a federal election across Ontario. Liberals charged that the government packed voters' lists with its own supporters. Indeed, voter numbers jumped by almost 40 percent over 1882, but the Conservative share of the poll in Ontario rose by just 0.3 percent. In Kingston, which Macdonald recaptured, the increase was from 1,686 to 2,728 — but he won by a mere seventeen votes. "We should have been beaten if we had not gone to the Country when we did."

The seventy-two-year-old prime minister felt "used up" by the campaign, but fresh challenges soon erupted. The fisheries clauses of the 1871 Treaty of Washington, which had permitted the Americans to fish along Canada's Atlantic coasts, lapsed in 1885. The Americans resented Canadian efforts to exclude them from inshore waters, and retaliated by claiming the Bering Sea as a private extension of Alaska. Unlike 1871, Canadians — Thompson and Tupper — led the tough negotiations which began in Washington in November 1887, backed by a senior British politician, Joseph Chamberlain. Shocked that the Americans attempted to treat Canada like a "country defeated after a great war," Chamberlain dismissed their negotiating team as "dishonest tricksters." "The Yankees are very bad neighbours," Macdonald lamented in January 1891.

No handover of power was possible until his two able lieutenants, Thompson and Tupper, returned from Washington, but in March 1888, Macdonald told Gowan, "we must make room for others," adding, in June, "I must shortly go." Yet, in contrast to earlier scares, his health seemed good. In particular, he looked well — "& shiny," Agnes noted in 1886. "I am in good health," he reported in 1887. In February 1889, Gowan found him "looking as young as ever," and Macdonald himself thought his health was "surprizingly good." In a sartorial gimmick, he had taken to wearing light-coloured suits and a jaunty white top hat, which added freshness to his characteristic good humour. Fifteen-year-old Maud Montgomery encountered him on Prince Edward Island in 1890, "a spry-looking old man — not handsome but pleasant-faced." (The silver-haired Agnes she thought "stately and imposing ... but not at all good-looking." Thompson, who disliked her, more bluntly commented, "ugly as sin.") A visitor to Ottawa that year watched Macdonald greeting callers to his office. Cracking jokes, "Sir John gave a skip" and "poked one of them in the ribs with his cane." Macdonald seemed "so bright and active ... he might have had a great many years before him."

There were no pensions for ex-ministers: Macdonald sometimes joked that he needed his $8,000 salary. During his illness in 1881, he had been sued for debt, but a well-wisher settled the case for $2,500. Challenged to explain the transaction, Macdonald

Courtesy of Library and Archives Canada/C-005327.

Maud Montgomery called Macdonald "a spry-looking old man — not handsome but pleasant-faced" when she met him on P.E.I. in 1890.

pleaded that he had borrowed the cash because "not being a rich man, I had not the money at the time." The *Globe* alleged a kickback from a railway contractor, but Macdonald insisted that he repaid the loan, in two instalments, and with interest. He also paid 7 percent annual interest on a $1,000 long-term loan from his sister Louisa, money that he assured her was soundly invested to make her rich "when I kick the bucket." By 1887, the fund had grown to $10,900: presumably the dividends easily covered the $70 a year that Louisa received. Macdonald purchased the Ottawa mansion "Earnscliffe" in 1883, but five years later he grumbled that renovations caused by dry rot "ruined" him. The bedrock of his finances was the $67,500 testimonial fund collected for him in 1871–72. Invested in six percent debentures, this yielded $4,050 a year — but in 1890 the bonds were refinanced at four percent, costing him $1,350 annually. "I must leave office ere long," he grumbled in January 1891, "& my income will be reduced": he wanted the capital invested in British Columbia mortgages, which paid seven percent.

In addition to Earnscliffe, insured in 1890 for $15,000, and the testimonial fund, Macdonald left $80,000 of his own money at his death — equal to the sum he had lost in 1869. There is no evidence for the subsequent rumour that his unexpected prosperity resulted from siphoning off political contributions for personal use. Macdonald's concern for his finances was understandable. His daughter, Mary, could never live an independent life: two full-time carers supported Agnes in looking after her, and much money was spent on unsuccessful medical treatment. To his credit, Macdonald neither exploited his handicapped daughter to win sympathy nor did he deny her existence: a wheelchair-access gallery at Earnscliffe enabled her to watch guests arriving for prime-ministerial dinner parties.

What might Macdonald do as an ex-prime minister? He cherished an impossible dream, to remain in the House of Commons, in alliance with Campbell in the Senate, to "take care of the Constitution." In fairness to any successor, Macdonald would have to leave Parliament — but what would he do and where would he live? Sometimes, he talked of writing political memoirs. He derided rumours that he might become governor general: "even if I had any aspirations, there is not the most remote chance of their being satisfied." Co-existing with the detested Mowat as lieutenant-governor of Ontario was impossible. British admirers hoped that Macdonald "would take his place in English society, which he was so well qualified to adorn." But London was an expensive city, and the British government would probably have named him to the House of Lords, an honour he could neither refuse nor afford. Tupper also wanted to make him a lord — and send him to Washington as British (and Canadian) ambassador.

Macdonald almost retired in the summer of 1888. "My only difficulty is about my successor," he told his secretary. Tupper refused the leadership, urging that it was Quebec's "turn" to provide Canada's prime minister. Hence Macdonald fell back on Hector Langevin: "there is no one else." Langevin wanted the job, but he was dragged down by bitter Quebec political feuding. The eventual compromise successor, the government's bilingual Senate leader, John Abbott, Macdonald thought unqualified. His senior colleagues had been subordinates for so long that it was hard to imagine any of them as a leader. Of the two possible younger candidates, fifty-one-year-old D'Alton McCarthy had refused even to join the Cabinet, while Thompson, fifty-two, was an abrasive Nova Scotian, "very able and a fine fellow," said Macdonald, but Ontario's vocal Protestants would not forgive his conversion to Catholicism.

In 1890, Macdonald's son Hugh thought there was "practically no Conservative Party in Canada," only "a very strong 'John A.' Party" which would disintegrate "when any one else attempts to take command." "All very well so long as you drive the coach but that cannot last for-ever," his friend Gowan commented in 1887. Once Macdonald departed, "then the danger comes of a smash up." Some pinned their hopes on divine intervention. Weeks before his death, a deferential bureaucrat assured Macdonald that the Almighty would not summon him "until He has prepared some one fit in some measure to assume your fallen mantle." In default of an obvious successor, it became tempting to assume that Macdonald would go on forever. "You'll never die, John A.!" a loyal supporter had once shouted. As testimony to the devotion he inspired, it was touching. As a political strategy, it represented myopic denial.

In June and July 1888, Canada's underground fires erupted anew. Premier Mercier suddenly cut through the long-running issue of Quebec's Jesuits' Estates, which legally belonged to the province but were morally the property of the Catholic Church. Mercier boldly ignored clerical quarrels over the distribution of the spoils, dividing the Estates among all possible stakeholders — even Quebec's Protestants were bought off. His master stroke was a provision that the act would take effect when "ratified by the Pope," which triggered knee-jerk Ontario demands to block this affront to Queen Victoria's authority. Mercier hurried to Ottawa to ask if his act would be disallowed. "Do you take me for a damn fool?" Macdonald responded. When the matter was raised in Parliament, he bluntly argued that the Quebec legislature "could do what they liked" with provincial property. Disallowance would trigger "the misery and the wretchedness" of religious and ethnic strife.

Only thirteen MPs voted for Ottawa to veto the Jesuits' Estates Act, but one of them was D'Alton McCarthy. No longer a potential leader, McCarthy almost bolted the party altogether. He encouraged the Manitoba government to ban French from its classrooms and stop funding Catholic schools: incomers from Ontario disliked the bicultural institutions established in 1870. Macdonald sidelined Manitoba Schools to the courts, but the Ottawa flames were fanned by another McCarthy campaign, to ban French as an official language in the future provinces of Alberta and Saskatchewan. By provoking conflict over language and religion, McCarthy had blocked Macdonald's chances of handing over either to Langevin, the Quebecker, or Thompson, the Catholic convert, whose sons attended a Jesuit boarding school in England. In any case, even in his mid-seventies, Macdonald was not going to be pushed. Late in 1889, an anonymous letter informed him that D'Alton McCarthy was alleging that the prime minister had lost his grip. Macdonald scribbled a confrontational endorsement: "Dear McCarthy, Who is your friend?" McCarthy, of course, backed off in embarrassment. Whatever their differences about Canada's future, "you were never in better form to lead your party than you are just now."

In March 1890 there came a further blow. J.-I. Tarte, a Quebec Conservative, briefed Macdonald about contract scams within Langevin's department, Public Works. Although Macdonald refused to censure his long-time ally — a Public Works contract in Kingston was less than pure — Langevin was no longer a possible prime minister. When Tupper returned to Ottawa in January 1891, Macdonald "looked up wearily from his papers" and greeted him: "I wish to God you were in my place." "Thank God I am not," Tupper replied. "We would all like to walk in your footsteps," Thompson wrote three months later, "but not in your shoes!" Only death would release Sir John A. Macdonald from office.

Macdonald now faced one last titanic electoral struggle. Wilfrid Laurier, Liberal leader since 1887, had responded to the yearning desire of Ontario farmers to sell their crops in the United States by endorsing "Unrestricted Reciprocity." Canada would drop its tariffs against American goods and produce, encouraging Washington to open its markets in return. Nobody explained why the Americans should act with such uncharacteristic generosity. A deluxe version of "U.R.," Commercial Union, committed Ottawa to adopting America's tariffs against the rest of the world, so that British and German goods could not enter the United States through the Canadian back door. To Macdonald, U.R. and "C.U." threatened the existence of an independent Canada itself. If five million Canadians integrated their economy with sixty-three million Americans, what would happen if the United States declared war on Britain? Canadians would be forced to choose between their prosperity and their allegiance. To Macdonald, "U.R. meant annexation."

At first, Macdonald assumed that U.R. "will be as dead as Julius Caesar" before the next election came round in 1892. But, in October 1890, Congress enacted the McKinley Tariff, targeting farm produce and pushing up America's already high import duties to new levels. It would be suicidal to campaign in rural Ontario once the 1891 harvest demonstrated to farmers their exclusion from American markets. Although he felt "the weight of 76 years greatly," in January 1891 Macdonald once again plunged Canada into a winter election. It was an unedifying campaign. "Nice chap" was his private assessment of Laurier, but publicly Macdonald accused the opposition of "veiled treason," branding all Liberals as annexationist plotters. His campaign slogan was "The Old Flag, The Old Policy, The Old Leader." The Old Leader only just survived the exhausting campaign. On a freezing February night, over-enthusiastic supporters paraded him through the streets of Napanee, where he had first run a law office almost sixty years earlier. By the time he arrived in Kingston, he was near collapse. His voice fell silent during the final week before polling day, on March 5, when the government was narrowly re-elected. Macdonald lost ground in central Canada, but secured a working majority from the "shreds and patches," as Ontario Liberals arrogantly termed the Maritimes and western Canada.

"I overworked myself during the campaign and forgot I was 76," Macdonald confessed. But when the new Parliament assembled, he taunted Laurier: "J'y suis, j'y reste" — here I am, here I stay. It was the only occasion he ever spoke French in the House. Six weeks later, he was dead. The campaign against Langevin destroyed Macdonald. On May 11, Parliament agreed to investigate Tarte's sensational charges of corruption in a Quebec dockyard contract. But there was a skeleton in Macdonald's own political cupboard. He had rewarded Kingston for re-electing him in 1887 by gifting the city a dry dock, to create jobs in ship repairing. The contract had gone to the lowest bidder, the unknown Andrew C. Bancroft, who had promptly formed a partnership with the Connolly brothers, experienced contractors — and also involved in the controversial Quebec project. Bancroft apparently signed the contract and definitely cashed the cheques, but the Connolly brothers built the dockyard. Costs steadily rose, and Public Works nodded through the increases. Bancroft was invisible because he did not exist. His invention was a device to hand the Kingston contract to the Connolly

Sir John A. Macdonald appeals to farmers and factory workers to save the National Policy in 1891. He barely survived the election campaign.

brothers. It defies belief that Macdonald, Kingston's MP, knew nothing of the scam. As Tarte unfolded his charges on May 11, 1891, Macdonald would have foreseen that he faced the same campaign of embarrassing accusations and shaming revelations that had unseated him in the 1873 Pacific Scandal. This time, aged seventy-six, there could be no way back from disgrace.

On May 12, the day after Tarte's bombshell, Sir John A. Macdonald suffered a stroke, so slight he hoped to disguise the episode even from Agnes. Indeed, Thompson thought him "well and bright again" when he returned to Parliament on Friday, May 22. However, that evening, his implacable foe Cartwright spoke with menacing sarcasm about Macdonald's generosity to Kingston, hinting at revelations regarding "Mr. Connolly." The House rose late but the prime minister lingered by his desk, as if instinct told him he would never return. Eventually, a colleague tactfully suggested it was "about time boys like you were home in bed." That weekend, Macdonald fell ill, and for the next two weeks, he fought for his life. "Condition hopeless," was the medical verdict on May 29, as a series of strokes gradually destroyed him.

Parliament, government, even Canada itself — all virtually went into abeyance. It was an odd succession crisis, for the two most obvious candidates, Thompson and Tupper, were determined to avoid the job. Despite his previous doubts, Macdonald had urged his colleagues to "rally around Abbott," but he had changed his mind when the Senate leader begged to be omitted from the Cabinet: Abbott was "too selfish" to lead. But, with Langevin politically wounded, Abbott became the compromise successor.

In the cities, bells announced that the battle was over. Minutes after Macdonald died at 10:15 p.m. on Saturday, June 6,

1891, they were mournfully tolling in Ottawa. Telegraph messages flashed across the country, and soon after eleven, the solemn peals broke out in Toronto. Genuine grief swept Canada, with headlines such as "Dead" in Qu'Appelle and "He Is Gone" in Victoria. The whole country paused for his funeral: at Brandon, even the locomotives were draped in mourning. John A. Macdonald was interred in Kingston, next to his mother "as I promised her that I should be there buried." Thirty years on, Helen still controlled her son.

In his tribute to Macdonald, opposition leader Laurier thought it "almost impossible" that Canada could "continue without him." Yet, curiously, Sir John A. was soon largely forgotten. Journalist Hector Charlesworth recalled that "to vast numbers of the community he seemed the prop which supported the whole structure of Canadian nationality." When his Dominion carried on without its creator, that mirage of Macdonald's indispensability was dissipated. Britain's Conservatives had built a

Macdonald's funeral united Canadians in grief. The massive procession leaves Ottawa's Parliament Hill on its way to Kingston.

million-strong campaigning organization, the Primrose League, on the memory of Disraeli, but nothing came of a proposal to form a Macdonald Guard to defend his ideals. His memory was discredited by the emerging tide of scandal. A month after Macdonald's death, the mythical Bancroft was exposed — although, like Macdonald himself, the Kingston contract scandal was hastily forgotten, especially by biographers. Although Abbott was only caretaker prime minister, in August he fired Langevin from Cabinet. "The Old Man's friends must feel ... that he was fortunate in his time of dying," the *Globe* cruelly remarked. "The most enthusiastic partisan of Sir John Macdonald would not attempt the hopeless task of defending his political morality," pronounced a British commentator. Instead, Macdonald's admirers entombed him in bronze across Canada: Hamilton unveiled the first statue, in 1893; Regina only raised enough funds to erect its joyless John A. in 1967. In Toronto's Queen's Park, a round-shouldered Sir John A. Macdonald seems weighed down by his imperial robes of the Order of the Bath. In cities across the country, he stared coldly at a Canada that no longer knew him. Despite five biographies, by 1921 he was "imperfectly, if at all, known" to contemporary Canadians.

Listening from the gallery that June day in 1891 as Canada's parliamentarians delivered emotional tributes, was a Halifax lawyer, visiting Ottawa on legal business. In 1911, Robert Borden would lead the Conservatives to victory, their first success in two decades. In twenty-four years, Macdonald won six elections — albeit narrowly in 1872. It took the Tories another 120 years, until Stephen Harper in 2011, to win their sixth majority government in the post-Macdonald era (plus a seventh in a wartime coalition sweep in 1917). Louis Riel had not risen from the grave, as he had foretold, but his ghost drove a wedge between the

Conservatives and Quebec. Initially, Macdonald was philosophical about this: "from a patriotic rather than from a party point of view, it is not to be regretted that the French should be more equally divided," he wrote in 1886. But throughout the twentieth century, French Canadians were not "equally divided," and the Conservatives paid the price for their weakness in Quebec with six federal minority governments between 1926 and 2008.

Macdonald himself ceased to be a potent political symbol. In his magnificent two-volume biography of 1952–55, Conservative intellectual Donald Creighton re-launched him as a Tory-nationalist icon, but the failure of the Diefenbaker government once again made Sir John A. a dated symbol, his British knighthood and his waving of the "Old Flag" irrelevant to the new bicultural Canada. In 1988, the next successful Conservative leader, Brian Mulroney, tore up the remnants of the "Old Policy" and took Canada into a continental trade deal, the strategy that Macdonald had denounced as treason a century before.

Academics talk of the "Macdonaldian" constitution, a centralizing straitjacket imposed in 1867, which crumbled against the reality of Canada's size and diversity. The picture is exaggerated. Macdonald intended the Dominion to be boss, but he never conspired to destroy the provinces — indeed, it was his constitution that the judges reinterpreted on looser, federal lines after 1883. Canada still endures the tensions between Ottawa control and provincial autonomy that first emerged in Macdonald's time, with the scope of government now extended into the wider battlefields of external relations, health, and welfare. Macdonald's 1867 constitution has changed much in spirit. No provincial legislation has been disallowed since 1943, the last British governor general went home in 1952, while the 1982 Charter of Rights and Freedoms shifted the balance of authority between Parliament and the courts. Yet Canada remains one of the few countries to be governed for a century and a half through the same basic document. Its truly "Macdonaldian" quality is its adaptability and capacity for compromise.

"There was in him some indescribable charm that acted by presence, seemingly without means or argument," commented a supporter. Macdonald's brother-in-law once remarked, "no one can know him long and not like him." Brown and Cartwright would have disagreed, but thousands of Canadians responded to his rare combination of "vivacity in social life linked to the coolest deliberation in affairs political." Yet the good humour and the approachability masked a complex personality. Macdonald's life was driven by his mother's determination that her surviving son should wipe out the humiliation of emigration. His father's continued business setbacks in Canada schooled him to cope with the mixed fortunes of politics. He would refer to "my usual desire to make the best of a bad state of things," urging voters that "we can't have all we want, and we must endeavor to get as nearly what we want as possible." He was in politics for the long term, not the quick fixes that some opponents naively thought possible. "My plan in life is never to give up," he wrote in 1864; "if I don't carry a thing this year I will next." His lonely schooldays left him with an enduring competitiveness. He fought, for the government, in 1837, a traumatic experience that he rarely mentioned, and he blamed that rebellion on an arrogant elite. In 1873 he boasted that "the old Family Compact tried to keep me down, but they couldn't." He was a moderate Conservative who fought extreme Tories, a compromiser who cried, as in 1885, "let us have peace." Once, in 1881, even Macdonald's sharpest critic had offered a sympathetic insight. "Putting the best possible construction on his political motive," observed the *Globe*, "it has been to carry on the government of the country somehow or other." Sometimes, governing Canada required dubious expedients.

In his forties, with his wife bedridden, his workload overwhelming, and his finances in trouble, the pressures triggered a midlife alcohol problem that intermittently erupted over two decades. But to remember someone who contributed so much to Canada merely as a drunk not only distorts the memory of John A. Macdonald but also dishonours the country that he did so much to create. Macdonald was not permanently intoxicated and his achievement was impressive even in the years when he struggled with his infirmity. As a later governor general, Lord Minto, commented, it is appropriate to recall Macdonald's alcohol problem if only because "he completely triumphed on this weakness."

We cannot know whether Confederation would have happened if he had never left Scotland, whether Canada would have expanded westward and built a railway to the Pacific had there been no John A. Macdonald. But, equally, we must not assume that others would have filled the gap with the same combination of personal skills and political judgment. "I have committed many mistakes," he admitted in 1882, "… there are many things I have done wrongly, and many things I have neglected that I should have done." Honest about his failures, he deserves the last word on his successes. "I have tried, according to the best of my judgment, to do what I could for the well-being of good government and future prosperity of this my beloved country."

Chronology

Macdonald and His Times	Canada and the World
1815	
	Battle of New Orleans, January 8. Last major clash between British and American armies in the War of 1812.
Born Glasgow, Scotland, January 11.	
	Battle of Waterloo, June 18. End of quarter-century of war between Britain and France.
1820 Family immigrates to Canada.	
1822 Death of Macdonald's brother, James.	
1825 Sent away from home to attend elite Kingston school.	

Macdonald and His Times	*Canada and the World*
1830 Becomes apprentice law clerk to George Mackenzie.	
1832 Manages law office at Napanee.	
1833 Manages law office at Hallowell.	
1834 Death of George Mackenzie.	
1835 Opens law office in Kingston.	
1836	Tories win flag-waving election in Upper Canada.
1837 Fights for government against W.L. Mackenzie's rebels.	Minor rebellions in Upper Canada, December.
1838 Shows his independence by taking unpopular cases.	Paramilitaries from USA attack Kingston area.
1839 Becomes a director of Kingston's Commercial Bank, and its legal adviser.	
1841 Campaign manager for J.R. Forsyth in Kingston election.	Upper and Lower Canada united, with Kingston as provincial capital.

Macdonald and His Times	*Canada and the World*
1842	
Takes vacation in Britain, becomes engaged to cousin Isabella Clark.	Reformers take control of ministry.
1843	
Elected Kingston Alderman.	Reformers move capital to Montreal.
Marries Isabella Clark.	
Forms law partnership with Alexander Campbell.	
	Governor Metcalfe forces Reformers to resign.
1844	
Elected to represent Kingston in provincial Assembly.	Narrow election victory for Tories on "loyalty" issue.
1845	
Isabella leaves Kingston for three-year absence in USA.	Threat of war between Britain and USA over Oregon boundary.
1846	
Appointment to Cabinet blocked by extreme Tories.	Britain adopts free trade, ending tariff preference on imports from Canada.
1847	
Appointed to Cabinet. Birth of son John Alexander.	
1848	
Defeat of ministry begins six years in opposition.	Election of Reform ministry.

Macdonald and His Times	*Canada and the World*
Death of John Alexander.	
1849	
	Montreal Tories burn parliament buildings, April.
Supports British American League to re-launch Conservative party, July.	Capital moved from Montreal, to alternate between Toronto and Quebec City.
Campbell ends law partnership.	
	Annexation Movement, October.
1850 Birth of son Hugh John.	
Visits Britain to secure investment in Trust and Loan Company.	
1853 Invests borrowed money in property boom.	
1854 Becomes attorney general West (justice minister for Upper Canada).	Sir Allan MacNab forms coalition of Conservatives and Hincksite Reformers.
Carries legislation to end clergy reserves.	
1856 Moves family to Toronto.	
Overwork and financial worries worsen alcohol problem.	

Macdonald and His Times	*Canada and the World*
Angry clash with George Brown.	
Reluctantly joins Cabinet revolt to oust MacNab.	
1857 Visits Britain as member of government delegation.	Choice of Canada's permanent capital referred to Queen Victoria.
Becomes premier November 26, calls elections, wins at Kingston by 1,189–9.	
Death of Isabella on December 28.	
1858 Struggles as premier, admits alcohol problem.	Stages tactical resignation, July.
	"Double shuffle" makes Cartier premier, August.
1859 Escapes drowning on Georgian Bay inspection tour.	
1860 Clash with Duke of Newcastle over status of Orange Order in Canada prevents Prince of Wales from visiting Kingston.	
Embarks on Upper Canada speaking tour to rebuild support.	

Macdonald and His Times	Canada and the World
1861	
	Outbreak of American Civil War.
Challenged at Kingston election by Oliver Mowat.	Census confirms Upper Canada has larger population than Lower Canada.
1862	
Defeat of Militia Bill and fall of Cartier ministry blamed on his alcohol problem.	Sandfield Macdonald becomes premier.
1864	
Joins Taché's minority ministry despite financial problems, March.	
	Great Coalition formed to tackle Canada's constitutional problems, June.
Leads arguments for Confederation.	Confederation agreed in principle at Charlottetown, September.
	Detailed scheme designed at Quebec Conference, October.
Seriously ill, November.	
1865	
	Defeat of Confederation in New Brunswick election, March.
Member of Canadian delegation to Britain to mobilize support for Confederation.	

Macdonald and His Times	*Canada and the World*
	Capital moves to Ottawa, September.
	Resignation of George Brown from Great Coalition, November.
1866	
	Fenian raid, May–June.
Toronto *Globe* denounces his alcohol problem; British government expresses concern.	
Chairs London Conference, December.	British North American delegates meet in London Conference to prepare Confederation legislation, December.
Badly injured in hotel fire, woos Agnes Bernard, December.	
1867 Negotiating skills impress British during Confederation talks.	
Marries Agnes Bernard, February.	British North America Act passed at Westminster, February–March.
First prime minister of the Dominion and knighted, July.	Dominion of Canada comes into being, July 1.
Unable to save Kingston's Commercial Bank, October.	

Macdonald and His Times	*Canada and the World*

1868
Overwork forces consideration
of resignation, February.

Visits Halifax to tackle Nova
Scotia discontent, August.

1869
Birth of daughter, Mary,
February.

Debts of $79,590.11 called in by
bank, April.

Métis block Ottawa's governor
William McDougall from entering
Red River, November.

1870
Globe renews denunciation of
alcohol problem, April.

Manitoba becomes fifth province.

Near fatal illness caused by
gallstone, May.

Métis leader Louis Riel confirms
death sentence on Thomas Scott.

1871
Member of imperial negotiating
team for Treaty of Washington.

British Columbia becomes
sixth province, with promise of
transcontinental railway within
ten years.

Liberals capture Ontario provincial government, December.

1872
Persuades Canadian Parliament
to accept Washington Treaty.

Macdonald and His Times	*Canada and the World*
Begins negotiations for contract to build Pacific Railway.	
Narrowly wins expensive Dominion election.	
	Pacific Railway contract awarded to Hugh Allan.
1873	
	"Pacific Scandal." Macdonald alleged to have sold Pacific contract for election funds, April to November.
	Prince Edward Island becomes seventh province.
Resigns, November.	Alexander Mackenzie forms Liberal government, November.
1874	
	Mackenzie wins large majority at election.
	Failure of negotiations for Reciprocity with USA.
1875	
Resists leadership bid by Alexander Galt.	Senate defeats Mackenzie's railway deal with British Columbia.
Moves to Toronto and resumes law practice.	

Macdonald and His Times	*Canada and the World*
1876 Supports protective tariff as part of "National Policy." Begins new form of campaigning, political picnics.	
1877 Tackles alcohol problem.	
1878 Becomes prime minister again, but defeated at Kingston.	General election returns Conservative government.
1879 Serious illness delays visit to Britain. Becomes "Right Honourable."	"National Policy" of tariff protection enacted.
1880	Pacific Railway contract awarded to George Stephen and Donald Smith, October.
1881 Visits Britain for rest and medical treatment after Ottawa doctor suspects cancer.	
1882	"Hiving of the Grits" redistribution of Ontario ridings. Conservatives re-elected.

Macdonald and His Times	*Canada and the World*
1883 Buys Ottawa mansion, "Earnscliffe."	
1884 Feted in Britain as imperial strong man.	Near-bankrupt CPR company mortgaged to Canadian government.
	Return of Louis Riel to Northwest.
1885	Renewed CPR funding crisis, February to June.
	Riel leads rebellion in Saskatchewan country, March to May.
	Franchise Act widens right to vote in Dominion elections.
	Last Spike completes transcontinental railway, November.
Confirms death sentence on Louis Riel.	Riel hanged for treason, November.
1886 Visits Western Canada.	Liberal government of Honoré Mercier takes office in Quebec.
1887 Gambles on February Dominion poll.	Conservatives win Dominion election.

Macdonald and His Times	*Canada and the World*
Re-elected for Kingston.	Beginning of tough negotiations with USA at Washington, November.

1888

Considers handing leadership to Hector Langevin.	Quebec legislature passes Jesuits' Estates Act.

1889

	Kingston awarded a dry dock, contract granted to non-existent A.C. Bancroft.
Refuses to disallow Quebec's Jesuits' Estates Act.	Ontario-based "Equal Rights Association" campaigns against special treatment for Catholic schools and French language.

1890

Refuses to act on warnings of corruption in Langevin's Public Works Department.	Demanding "community of language among the people of Canada," D'Alton McCarthy calls for end to official status for French in North West Territories (future Alberta and Saskatchewan), January.
	Manitoba Public Schools Act ends funding to denominational schools, challenged in courts.
	US Congress increases import duties in McKinley Tariff, October.

1891

Paints Liberal opposition as pro-American traitors during election campaign, January–March.	

Macdonald and His Times	*Canada and the World*
Collapses, February 24.	
	Conservatives win general election, March 6.
Suffers minor stroke, May 12.	Langevin charged in Parliament with corruption, May 12.
Last appearance in Parliament, May 22.	
Death, June 6.	
	John Abbott becomes prime minister, June 16.

Note on Sources

Sources are given in short form, relying upon Internet searches and computerized library catalogues for full identification. Publications are indicated by author/editor and year, with keywords for clarification. Major sources available online in September 2012 are asterisked (*) but many require subscription. Many books and articles are also available online.

The chief archival source for the life of John A. Macdonald remains his papers (gradually coming online*) in Library and Archives Canada (LAC, Ottawa), discussed by Martin, *Journal of Historical Biography**, 2006. LAC also holds the Gowan papers, plus diaries of Agnes Macdonald and Edmund Meredith. The Ontario Archives (Toronto) holds the papers of Alexander Campbell (excellent calendar*) and T.C. Patteson.

For Macdonald's correspondence: Pope, 1921*; Johnson, 1968 (for 1836–57); Johnson and Stelmack, 1969 (for 1858–61). For family letters, Johnson, *Affectionately Yours*, 1969.

For speeches, *Address*, 1861; Pope, *Confederation Documents*, 1895/ Browne, 1969; *Confederation Debates*, 1865/Waite, 1963, 2006; Whelan/Harvey, *Union ... Provinces*, 1927; *Dominion Campaign*, 1882; *Speech ... Ottawa*, 1886. Parliamentary debates are available to 1856, and from 1874*.

Complete files survive of the Toronto *Globe** and Victoria *Colonist**. Other newspapers are available through Google News Archive (e.g., partial runs of the Toronto *Mail* and Montreal *Gazette*)*, Paper of Record*, Manitobia* and Peel's Prairie Provinces (University of Alberta)*.

For an overview of Macdonald's life, Johnson and Waite, *Dictionary of Canadian Biography*, ix (1990)*. Major biographies include Pope (1894)*, Creighton (1952/1955), and Gwyn (2007/2011). Pope published extensive documentation.

For anecdotes and insights, Biggar (1891*/Smith and McLeod, 1979); Macpherson, 1891*; Adam, 1891*; Pope, *Day*, 1920*; Waite, in Dyck and Krosby, *Empire and Nations*, 1969; Waite, *Life and World*, 1975; Phenix, 2006.

For Macdonald's finances, Johnson ("Young Non-Politician," Canadian Historical Association *Annual Report*, 1971). For his part in the 1837 rebellion, Johnson, *Ontario History*, 1968. For his alcohol problem, Martin, *Journal of Canadian Studies*, 2006. For his relations with Kingston, Johnson, Livermore, and Swainson in Tulchinsky, *To Preserve and Defend* (1976) and Martin, *Favourite Son?*, 2011. For Macdonald as premier in 1857–58, Martin, *British Journal of Canadian Studies*, 2007. For his 1885 Franchise Act, Stewart, "Greatest Triumph," *Canadian Historical Review*, 1982. For his Canadian accent, Martin, *British Journal of Canadian Studies*, 2004.

For Macdonald's disqualification at Kingston in 1874, Brady, "Sinners and Publicans," *Ontario History*, 1984, and his similar experience in Lennox in 1883, Eadie, *Ontario History*, 1984.

Useful biographies include studies of Agnes Macdonald (Reynolds, *Agnes*, 1990); George Brown (Careless, 1959, 1963); George Cartier (Young, 1981); Alexander Galt (Skelton, 1920/MacLean, 1966); Edmund Head (Kerr, 1954); Luther Holton (Klassen, 2001); Joseph Howe (Beck, 1983); Hector Langevin (Désilets, 1969); Sandfield Macdonald (Hodgins, 1971); D'Arcy McGee (Wilson, 2011); Alexander Mackenzie (Thomson, 1960); Allan MacNab (Beer, 1984); Oliver Mowat (Evans, 1992); Joseph Pope (Pope, 1960); Donald A. Smith (McDonald, *Strathcona*, 1996); George Stephen (Gilbert, 1965/1976); John Thompson (Waite, *Man from Halifax*, 1985); Charles Tupper (Saunders, 1916). Macdonald's contemporaries appear in *Dictionary of Canadian Biography**.

Also useful are the diaries of Robert Harrison (Oliver, *Conventional Man*, 2003) and the correspondence of Lord Elgin (Doughty, 1937) and Lord Dufferin (de Kiewiet and Underhill, 1955). Cartwright's *Reminiscences* (1912) were hostile but insightful. An embittered memoir by Macdonald's New Brunswick colleague Peter Mitchell was published by Burt in *Canadian Historical Review*, 1961*.

For Dominion election results, Beck, *Pendulum of Power* (1968) and for Ontario, Evans, *Mowat*.

For bibliographies, Swainson, 1969, and Martin, *Favourite Son?*, which lists many useful articles published by *Historic Kingston*.

Index